THE RHIND LECTURES IN ARCHÆOLOGY

IN CONNECTION WITH

THE SOCIETY OF ANTIQUARIES OF SCOTLAND

Delivered in December, 1889, on the

EARLY ETHNOLOGY OF THE BRITISH ISLES

BY

JOHN RHYS, M.A.
Professor of Celtic at Oxford

Facsimile reprint
published in 1990
by Llanerch Enterprises.
ISBN 0947992 48 0.

AS PRINTED IN *THE SCOTTISH REVIEW*
FOR APRIL, 1890—JULY, 1891.

THE EARLY ETHNOLOGY OF THE BRITISH ISLES.

THE Celtic nations of the present day consist, ethnologically speaking, partly of Aryans and partly of the non-Aryan races which the Aryans found inhabiting the countries invaded by them in prehistoric times. So it will be convenient on the whole to treat of them under these two heads, and to begin with them from their Aryan side, inasmuch as the Aryans are better known than the earlier inhabitants.

For the proofs that the Celts are Aryan in speech one has only to open any comparative grammar or vocabulary of the Aryan languages; but the question what precisely is to be understood by the term Aryan has of recent years much occupied the student of language; and still more has he been exercised by the kindred question, whence the Aryans set out to conquer those portions of the globe of which they are now lords. The Muse of the older Philology was loth to fix on any locality very far away from the Garden of Eden. In time, however, she was forced to wander from one spot to another, though she clave to the East all the while; and when she had obeyed the supposed behests of science so far as to locate the Aryan incunabula in a distant non-Aryan land in Central Asia, she fondly imagined that she had found a permanent resting place; but, alas! the curse of research was upon her, for she must now quit the East where she had long cherished the one-sided motto, *Ex Oriente Lux*, and roam over Europe in quest of the primitive home of Aryan man. These her wanderings have not yet come to an end, but the probability of her returning to the East is growing feebler daily, as the conviction is steadily gaining ground among scholars, that the great European race is of European origin and not an immigrant from the stagnant East. To be brief, one may say that the regions which have gained most favour in this respect are Scandinavia and North Germany, or the neighbourhood of the Baltic Sea.

Our business here, however, is to try to understand what is meant by Celtic, and how the Celtic nations of the present day stand in respect of one another. As the data which I propose to deal with are of a linguistic nature, I must confine myself in the first instance to the narrower question of the mutual relations of the Celtic languages. Now it is a commonplace of our glottology that the Neoceltic dialects divide themselves into two groups: a Goidelic group, embracing the Celtic idioms of Ireland, Man, and Scotland; and a Brythonic group, embracing those of Wales, Cornwall, and Brittany. With regard to the former, there is a tendency in Scotch and English parlance, as you know, to confine the word Gaelic to the Gaelic of Scotland, and to forget that Irish and Manx are equally Gaelic, that those terms are in fact merely the shorter names for Irish Gaelic and Manx Gaelic. So it has been thought expedient to go back to the older native form of the word Gael, and fashion another adjective Goidelic, to cover the three great dialects of Gaelic, Irish Gaelic, Manx Gaelic, and Scotch Gaelic. Now the older form of Gael (written in Gaelic *Gaidheal*, and pronounced with a *dh* which is not heard) was Goidel or Gaidel, whence the technical term Goidelic has been coined. It may be mentioned in passing that the original meaning of the word Goidel or Gael is utterly unknown; but I would entreat you not to connect it with Gaul or Gallia and the Galli of that country in Roman times: Gael, standing as it does for Goidel, has absolutely nothing to do with the Gallus and Gallia of classical authors. With regard to the term Brythonic as the name for the other group, it would be still more inconvenient and misleading to speak of the Welsh, the Cornish, and the Bretons as Britannic or British, seeing that those adjectives lead off with connotations of their own. So recourse has here also been had to the native vocabulary, according to which the Welsh word for a Briton, Latin Britto, is Brython 'a Briton or Welshman;' and the language of the peoples of this group is termed in Welsh Brythoneg, one of the names also of the Welsh language, while in Cornish and Breton, it is Brethonec and Brezonec, meaning those dialects respectively: Brython in its various forms is to be regarded as the national name of all this group, as Goidel or Gael is of the other. Briefly, you have to classify the Celts of the present day into Goidels and Brythons: at the one pole you have your Gaels of the Highlands, and at the other my countrymen in Wales; and you will be proof against the fascination of much of the nonsense talked of the Celts, if you will always bear in mind that Gaels and Welshmen are no less unintelligible to one another, to say the least of it, than would be the inhabitants of Edinburgh and Berlin.

This classification is dictated by the phonology of the Neoceltic languages, as illustrated by two or three very obvious differences. One of the most palpable of these differences is presented to us in the fact that the Goidels have retained a guttural, where the Brythons have labialized it into another kind of consonant. Take for instance *macc* or *mac*, which is the word for boy and son in all the Goidelic dialects. The genitive of this word as found in the early Ogam inscriptions of Ireland, was *maqui*, which would have been in early Brythonic *mapi*, and the Old Welsh form for all cases was in fact *map* (now *mâb*) 'boy or son;' and we can trace the *q* in a derivative word which carries us back to the time of the Roman occupation, namely, in *mabon*, 'a child or boy,' a word applied in old Welsh poetry to the infant Jesus. This word mabon in its ancient form of Mapon, is applied to a Celtic god called in Latin, Apollo Maponus, on a fine monument of pagan piety at Hexham. He was so called, doubtless, in reference to the perennial youthfulness of the Celtic Apollo: this kind of hero of Celtic stories is, I may mention in passing, a great and formidable warrior when he is only seven years old. But what I wish you clearly to understand is, that the word which was *maqui* in Early Goidelic must have been *mapi* in Early Brythonic, that the same difference extends to other words, and that it dates before the dawn of Celtic history. So far I have only instanced a consonant, and this will probably call to your minds Voltaire's definition of etymology as the science in which the vowels did not matter at all, and the consonants very little. There used to be some truth in that, but of late the vowels of the Aryan languages have been so minutely studied that the whole subject of Aryan philology has within the last few years been completely revolutionized, and that we have all had to practice, so to say, a new scale, a subtle chromatic scale as compared with the very easy one in which the older philologists eternally harped on the same three notes, *a*, *i*, *u*. This difficult exercise has recently proved the means of spoiling several good tempers, for nothing could be more trying for men wont to discourse genially and elegantly on the simplicity of early Aryan institutions, language included, than to find this simplicity to be mainly of their own cerebration. In deference then to the recently established importance of Aryan vowels, I must give you a vocalic instance to place alongside of the consonantal one to which I have just alluded, but I will only mention the tendency which the Brythons had in certain periods of their history to narrow a long *u* into a long *i*, or to a sound somewhat resembling the French *u* of *une*, and other words of the same class. The Goidelic word for a dog or hound will do for our purpose. It is, as many of you doubtless know, *cū* (genitive *con*) which is the same word as the English *hound*, and its *u* is represented by the *ou* of the English word, but in Welsh the vowel has been unrounded into *ī*, the Welsh word being *cī*. I may mention in passing that you have a form of *cū* in the name of the neighbouring town of Linlithgow, which means the lake of *Liathchū* or Grey Dog; the word appears to occur also with the correct Goidelic genitive as *Linliathchon*; and on the other side of the island we have the name of the great city of Glasgow, which is probably but a modified pronunciation of *Glaschū*, one of Kentigern's Gaelic names, meaning likewise the Grey Dog or Hound: his other names appear to have been *Munchū* (made into Mungo) usually supposed to mean 'Dear Dog,' and *Deschū*, which may have meant Southern Hound. In the mouth of a Brython Glaschū would become Glasgi, but whether the pronunciation 'Glasgic' is or is not to be traced back to the Welsh of Strathclyde, or to a more modern lightness of pronunciation natural to a 'Glasgie body,' I must leave you to decide. Other instances are plentiful, however, such as the Goidelic *dūin*, 'a fort or stronghold,' which is familiar to you in a modified pronunciation in such names as Dundas, Dundee, and last but not least Dunedin. Now this *dūin* is in Welsh *dīn*, whence a synonymous *dinas*, 'a town or city.' The tendency to this difference of pronunciation seems also to date very early, and as a sort of *memoria technica* I might give you names like Mac Iain of Dundas as representing the Goidel, and Bevan of Dinmael as representing the Brython; both Mac Iain and Bevan mean in the the last resort John's Son, the Welsh having been curtailed successively, mab Iouann, vap Ievan, vab Ivan, Ab Ivan, B-Ivan, Bevan, just as in the Isle of Man the word *mac* has been reduced to the initial *c* of such names as Claig or Cleg, 'Son of the *Liag* or Physician,' and Mac Iain itself appears there as Keoin.

From the equivalence of the *c* of *mac* with the *p* (or *b*) of *map* (or *mab*) you are not to suppose that there has been any confusion of gutturals and labials, or to assume with the charlatans always to be found in the Celtic field, that Goidelic *c* interchanges with Brythonic *p*: nothing of the kind. What really happens with regard to the word *mac* is, that the old pronunciation with a *qu* has been simplified by dropping the second element of the combination: that is the Goidelic treatment. The Brythonic treatment was different: the combination *qu* consisting of a guttural followed by a labial, was made entirely labial and simplified into *p*. So when you meet with a Goidelic word with *c* corresponding to a Welsh one with *p*, you are not to predicate the interchange of *c* and *p*, but the former presence of a *qu*, which the Goidel has made into *c* and the Brython into *p*. In both *map* and *din* the Brython gets rid of the rounded sounds of *u* and *ū*, and in this he shows an early departure from original Aryan speech. On these and similar grounds one is warranted in classifying the Celtic languages of modern times as Goidelic and Brythonic, and the distinction can be extended back into the distant past; but that raises another question, which must now be briefly mentioned.

When one passes to the Continent and begins to ask after the affinities of ancient Gaulish the subject of classification comes again to the foreground. The remains of old Gaulish consist of a few inscriptions and a considerable number of proper names occurring in the works of Greek and Latin writers; but they suffice to prove that Gaulish goes with Brythonic and not with Goidelic, so that instead of a Brythonic group we may now speak of a Gallo-Brythonic group. Such Gaulish names as the following are in point, *Eporedorix*, which involves a word *epos* corresponding to the Goidelic *eoch* 'a horse,' Latin *equus*; and *Pennowindos*, in Welsh Penwyn, meaning white-headed, which would have been in early Goidelic *Quennowindos* since it appears later as Cennfind. Here and there, however, in lands occupied by the Continental Celts one comes across names with qu such as Sequana 'the Seine' and that of the people called Sequani; possibly *Aquitani* was likewise a Celtic word. Such names as these would seem to suggest that there was at one time a Celtic people on the Continent whose language resembled the dialects of the Goidelic group. This raises several questions, not the least pressing of which is how such a people should be designated.

Before, however, turning our attention to that question, it would be well to look what further evidence there is of the existence of Q Celts on the Continent. In the first place it may be mentioned, that the Q Celts of the British Isles doubtless came here from the Continent, and that their migration probably took place only after the race to which they belonged had long obtained possession of the coast opposite Britain. It may be added that history does not on the whole lead one to expect those Celts of the Continent to have come over here in a body, leaving their Continental home empty: some of them doubtless remained behind, probably the great bulk of them. In a word it is morally certain that at some distant epoch the seaboard of Europe from Holland to Spain was in part occupied by Celts of the Q group. In the next place a writer of the fourth century, Sulpicius Severus, speaks in one of his dialogues of Celtic and Gallic: the words in point occur in Dialog. I. 27, and run thus: " Tu uero, inquit Postumianus, uel Celtice, aut si mauis, Gallice loquere, dummodo jam Martinum loquaris." From this it is natural to infer that two languages called respectively Celtic and Gallic were still in use in Sulpicius's time, and his mention of them deserves all the more consideration as he is said to have belonged to a good family in Aquitania, where if anywhere on the Continent one might expect the Celtic here in question to have survived. We have perhaps a stronger argument than that of any single passage, such as the one cited, in the existence of the two names Galli and Celtæ with their respective adjectives. Till comparatively recently these words used to be regarded as synonymous throughout, but the tendency of modern research is decidedly to treat them as originally referring to two different sets of Celts. Some help to distinguish them may be derived from the writings of Julius Cæsar. He regarded Gaul as divided into three parts, one of which was occupied by the Aquitani, who dwelt beyond the Garonne. These last were probably wholly or in great part non-Celtic and non-Aryan, while the other two were doubtless mainly Celtic. These were the Celtæ and the Belgæ respectively. The Celtæ according to Cæsar were so called in their own language, while the Romans spoke and wrote of them in common with the other peoples of Gaul as Galli, and the whole country was called from them Gallia, a name which in passing through French has assumed the form Gaule in that language, whence the English *Gaul*. As to the locality of the people who called themselves Celtæ, Cæsar tells us that they were separated from the Aquitani by the Garonne and from the Belgæ by the Seine and the Marne; that is to say we are left to gather that the Celtæ occupied all

Gaul from the Garonne to the Seine and its tributary, in other words, all central and north-western France, in so far as that tract was Celtic at all. Cæsar, it will be seen, had to use his word Galli in two senses, one restricted and one more general, as already indicated; and we should be doing similarly with the words Celt and Celtic, if we applied them specially to the people who called themselves Celtæ, and if at the same time we followed the modern usage of applying them to the whole Aryan branch, embracing peoples of both groups, corresponding to Goidelic and Brythonic in these islands. To avoid this it is, perhaps, best to have recourse to a special name for the Celtæ in the narrower sense, and since Roman authors had on the whole a tendency to term their country Celtica, that is, to restrict the use of that term to the territory of the Celtæ, one may venture to call the inhabitants Celtica is, for which we have the analogy of Africans and Americans. But beyond the Celtica of Cæsar's time, the Celticans probably formed the bulk of the Aryan population within that tract of southern Gaul out of which the Romans had carved their Province. At any rate, that may be supposed to apply to the time anterior to the conquest of the Allobroges, who probably belonged to the other Celtic group. The Celticans had also penetrated, it would seem, into Spain, where their presence is attested by the well-known name of the mixed people of the Celtiberians. The third division of Gaul, according to Cæsar's account, was that inhabited by the Belgæ to the east and north-east of Celtica; but Cæsar's Belgæ are also to be regarded as the Galli proper, or else we have to add to the Belgæ certain peoples who were the Galli proper, in order to fill the map of ancient Gaul as outlined by him. It is needless to discuss the old-fashioned view that the Belgæ were Teutons and not Celts, for this would have to be maintained in the teeth of the whole glottological evidence; and it may be relegated to the same limbo as the groundless conjecture which would connect the Belgæ with the mythic folk of the Fir Bolg of ancient Erinn. It will suffice for the present to have roughly indicated the lines to be insisted on. Our data lead one to classify the Celts, looked at from a linguistic point of view, into (1) a P Group, comprising the Brythons of modern times and the Galli of antiquity—let us comprehensively term them Gallo-Brythonic, or perhaps better, Brytho-Gallic; and (2) a Q Group, including the Goidelic Celts of our day and the ancient Celticans of the Continent: this might be comprehensively called Goidelo-Celtican.

We have now to endeavour to form some idea of the relation of these two sets of Celtic peoples to one another, and our attention is first attracted by their geographical position; but here enters the question of the original home of the Aryans in the form of the narrower question, whence the Celts came to the lands where we find them. This, however, matters little, as no scholar seems prepared to maintain that they issued originally from Ireland or the West of Scotland, or that they swarmed across from Africa into Spain and Gaul. Roughly speaking, the march of the early Celts may be assumed to have been towards the West and the South. Wherever, then, subject to this limitation, they started from, you find that as a rule those of the Q group occupy the furthest portions of the area from the point of departure. Thus you have them in the west and south of Gaul, and in Spain, in Ireland also, and the Islands and Highlands of Scotland. In other words, the Q Celts were clearly here before those of the other group, and it is but natural to suppose that the latter came as invaders, who partly drove the earlier comers before them and partly subjugated them. Under these conditions a state of things arose, which had not passed away in Gaul in the time of Cæsar, for he makes us acquainted with the numerous retinues which the Gaulish nobles gathered round them of clients and debtors. All that points to a population consisting of a numerically small ruling class of conquerors, with the bulk of the inhabitants enslaved by them. The ruling class was the Gauls, and their enslaved subjects, in so far as they were Celts, were the Celticans. The Romans, when they came on the scene, informed their countrymen mostly about the ruling Gauls, and troubled themselves little about the subject race. Nor for our purpose would that be all, for it is by no means improbable that Celtican names were learned by Roman and Greek travellers mostly from Gaulish mouths, in which they underwent serious modifications, if not wholesale translation. Not many proper names, therefore, of a distinctively Celtican description are to be expected; nevertheless, a few such occur in Roman inscriptions, especially from Spain and Portugal, from the South of France, from the neighbourhood of the Alps and the North of Italy. I must, however, not trouble you with the details and the abstruse questions of language which they suggest. I will only mention one name of a place, given in the Antonine Itinerary, as situated between Lisbon and Merida in Portugal: it is Equabona, which reminds one of such Celtic place-names as Bononia, now Boulogne and Bologna, and as Vindobona, now Vienna; but Equabona was not Gaulish, for in that language it would have been Epobona, like Eporedia and the like. The probability is that it was Celtican with its first element, *equa*, of the same origin as the Latin word *equus*, 'horse,' Irish *ech*, 'a horse.' The Welsh form, on the other hand, was *ep*, which occurs in the word *epaul*, 'a colt,' now reduced in that language to *ebol*.

Now I have just skimmed over the question of the Celtic peoples of the west of Europe, including these islands; I have had to pass over most of the details lest I should weary you with minute points of philology of which you could scarcely judge without having them clearly stated in black and white, so as to be studied at leisure. In the British Isles we distinguish two groups of Celts, an older one called the Goidelic, and a later one the Brythonic. To the former belong, linguistically speaking, the *macs* of Scotland, of Man and of Erinn; and to the latter the Bowens and Bevans, the Powels and Pryses of Wales, and their kinsmen in Cornwall and Little Britain. I have further mentioned some reasons and hinted at others for believing that the Celts of the Continent, in ancient times, were similarly distinguished among themselves, the Gauls being of the same group as the Brythons, and the Celticans of the same group as the Goidels. The Brythons and the Gauls make up one larger group, which I have ventured to term briefly, P Celts, while the Celticans and Goidels make up another, which may be similarly termed Q Celts. Add to this that the Q Celts, the *macs*, so to say, were the first comers, and that the P Celts must have been later intruders, and you have the sum and substance of what I have so far tried to set forth.

This classification, however, of the Celts into a Q and a P group is not to be dismissed without reference to the like classification of certain other Aryans of Europe. Thus the Romans had qu in their language just as the ancient Irish had, but the Romans stood nearly alone in Italy in this respect; for all the other dialects, collectively spoken of as Oscan and Umbrian, belonged to the labializing or P Group. The Italians using Latin at the opening of the pages of Roman history, occupy a comparatively small area. It had probably been greatly narrowed by the other Italians, especially the Sabines, by whom Roman legend shows early Rome hard pressed. The Faliscan dialect, spoken by the people of Falerii, was closely akin to Latin, although Falerii was situated in Etruria. The meaning of that seems to be that it was a remnant of a population of the same stock as the Romans, and occupying the country which the Etruscans had seized upon, and levelled of its linguistic landmarks, with the exception of this spot, which, for some reason or other, successive invasions had not obliterated. Further, the remains of the oldest Sicilian dialects are supposed to show traces of close resemblance to Latin, a circumstance which suggests that Latin, or dialects of the same group, once extended along the western coast as far as Sicily. Their disappearance from most of that tract was due probably to the conquests made by peoples of the Oscan name. Behind the Oscans came pressing southwards the kindred people of the Umbrians, who continued to occupy a great part of the eastern coast of Italy until the coming of the Senones and other Gaulish tribes, who robbed them of a portion of their territory, and before this the Umbrians had been deprived of portions of their possessions by the non-Aryan race of the Etruscans. In other words, the Italians of the Q group were in Italy before the other group, and spoke dialects which we may briefly call Siculo-Latin. These latter continued to exist in Latium, and left remnants of their existence at Falerii and in Sicily. The peoples of the Siculo-Latin Q group were followed into Italy by the Aryans of the P group, known as Oscans and Umbrians, who appear to have occupied the whole width of the peninsula behind the Q Italians, and also made their way south along the east of the peninsula. Thence by degrees they took possession of the greater part of the western coast south of Latium, and even penetrated into Sicily, where traces of an Oscan dialect is known to history as that of the Mamertini. As a help to remember the phonological distinctions between the Celts, I have suggested the *macs* of the Goidel and the *Powels* and *Bevans* of the Welsh; so when we have to do with Italy, you may remember Pontius Pilate as representing the Osco-Umbrian branch, with Pontius for Pomptius, derived from *pomptos*, 'fifth'; for had his name been purely Latin it would have been Quinctius or Quintius: so Quintius and Pontius may serve as key words. But what I want you particularly to notice is that the Q people, the Quintiuses, came into Italy first, and that the P people, the Pontiuses, arrived later, just as the Celtic people of the Q group, the Goidelic *macs*, arrived first in Celtic lands, while the P Celts only came some time later.

A similar remark may be made concerning Greece, where the gutturalizing Greeks are most obviously represented by the dialect which Herodotus wrote, with such forms as κῶs and κότερος, for the πῶs and πότερος of the more common dialects. Herodotus was a native of Halicarnassus, and it is highly probable that the Greek which Herodotus wrote, or Greek closely resembling it, belonged to Asia Minor. Halicarnassus was sometimes described as a colony of Trœzen, and sometimes of Argos; but the dialect was Ionian. In other words, it was a dialect spoken originally by Greeks of the Ionic group, who probably represented the oldest Aryan settlers of the Hellenic world, as may be gathered from the fact of the so-called return of the Heraclidæ, as representing the victorious advance of the Dorians, the later comers. . But in Greece the fusion of the dialects, as presented to us in Greek literature, is found so far advanced that no such hard and fast line can be drawn between them as among the Italians and the Celts: all we can with certainty infer is, that the same division into a Q and a P group once obtained in the Hellenic world. But we may add, with great probability, that the Greeks of the Q group, pushed as they were to Asia and the islands, formed the first comers, while the P Greeks as represented by the Dorians came later to conquer and displace them. Lastly the scanty remains of the languages spoken by the Thracians and the Phrygians of antiquity would seem to warrant the inference that the same linguistic distinction applied among them likewise. The researches of your learned and indefatigable countryman, Professor Ramsay, have led him to regard the Phrygians as Europeans who entered Asia Minor across the Hellespont, and to see in Phrygians and Carians " two very closely kindred tribes, nearly related to some of the Greek races." These Phrygio-Carians were a conquering race and a similar ruling caste of the same stock existed in Lydia and Lycia. Such is Prof. Ramsay's conclusion, and it harmonizes on the whole with the views of those who, rightly or wrongly, regard the Armenians as representing the ancient inhabitants of Phrygia. For the case admits of being put thus: the Phrygio-Carian conquerors were Aryans of the P Group, while the Armenians linguistically belonged to the Q Group: the latter may therefore be provisionally treated as representing those of the inhabitants of Asia Minor who, dwelling in the mountain regions, escaped the Phrygio-Carian conquest, and thereby preserved their language free from any admixture of the features characteristic of Aryan speech of the P Group.

These remarks suggest two considerations, namely that of the fusion of nations of the P and the Q groups with one another as already defined in part, and that of the closer community of origin of those of the P group. Let us take the latter first: put into the form of a question it would be this—does the change of qu into p prove that the p dialects are to be regarded as of a common descent within the Aryan family? The answer to this must be that in itself it does not, as the change is possibly of such a nature that it may take place in any language which happens to have the combination *qu*; but then we are entitled to ask why we should have it three or four times over in a certain portion of the Aryan world and not at all in the rest of it. Irish, Latin, and certain dialects of Greek remained, as far as concerns the guttural, on the level, roughly speaking, of Sanskrit, Zend, Slavonic and Teutonic, as you will at once perceive by examining any instance in point, such as the interrogative pronoun, which is in Sanscrit *ka*, in Gothic *hva* and in English *who*. Compare with these the Irish *cia* 'who,' Latin *qui*, the Herodotean κοῖος, κότερος and the like. No phonologist supposes the change to have been from *p* to *qu* but from *qu* to *p*. Goidelic, therefore, and Latin, together with the Greek in question, are in this respect practically on the ancient level of Aryan speech, while the labializing must be regarded as an exception introduced by the later Aryan invasion represented by the Gallo-Brythons, the Osco-Umbrians, the Doric Greeks and the Phrygio-Carian conquerors of Asia Minor. Why then should we have all these three or four instances of the exceptional treatment in the inner area alone of only one portion of the Aryan world? The impossibility of answering this question brings us forcibly back to the suggestion of a common origin of all the P peoples; for that hypothesis relieves one of the necessity of postulating the labilization of *qu* three or four times independently in as many countries. Once will suffice, if we may suppose, as I think we may, that the P nations swarmed forth from the same home. We arrive at the same conclusion by reckoning the chances of the change of *qu* into *p* occurring so many times within the same area: stated at their lowest calculation they prove to be no less than 5 to 1 against it, that is to say in favour of the hypothesis here advanced that the people of the P group set out from a common home after their common language had once for all made the change here in question. As a corollary to this it may be suggested that the common home in question stood somewhere in the Alpine region of central Europe. Some such a spot would best satisfy the requirements of the theory, and, looked at from that point of vantage, the territory taken possession of by Aryans of the P group would form a smaller area within a larger one belonging to populations of the Q group of the same stock, and the descent of the Dorians into the Balkan peninsula becomes a part of a larger movement of the P Aryans, that is to say, of a movement which resulted in giving new inhabitants to Italy and Gaul, and through the latter to Spain and Britain.

Granted this, we are provided with a key to a variety of difficulties presented by the Celtic, Italian, and Hellenic tongues; and we are brought back to the other question, namely, that of the fusion of the two groups of Aryans in the lands here in point. Here language must again serve as our guide, for to understand the extent of any such fusion of language of the Q and P groups, we have to help us those Aryan languages which have been submitted to no influence of the P group — such, for instance, as Teutonic, Slavonic, and Sanskrit. Now, of the Western groups showing the influence of the P group, the least affected by it may be said to be decidedly Latin. The case of Latin is a very remarkable one: after being pressed within a small area, it began to conquer all the dialects around it, nor stopped till it became one of the great languages of civilization. The point to be specially noticed is the fact, that the antagonism between the ancient Romans and the Osco-Umbrian peoples in their neighbourhood was so intense, that the Latin language preserved itself comparatively free from the influence of the P dialects up to the period of its classical literature. Thus does Latin not only agree with the rest of the Q dialects in retaining the surd guttural of the combination *qu*, but also in not labialixing the corresponding *gu* into *b*, as one finds done in Irish and in Greek. Latin either retains the combination or simplifies it more frequently into *v* by dropping the *g*. Take, for instance, the Latin *unguo* 'I smear,' Alemannic *anche* 'butter,' and contrast with them the Irish *imb* 'butter' and Welsh *ymenyn*, from an early form *imben;* take also the Latin *venio* 'I come,' for *guenio*, of the same origin as the English word come, and contrast the Greek form βαίνω, 'I walk.' A remarkable exception to the usual homogeneity of the Latin vocabulary is the word *bos* 'an ox,' which is probably a loan-word from Oscan: in Latin it would have been *vos*, or at any rate begin with a *v*. To leave the subject of exceptions, another point on which Latin has remained on the old level is that of long *u*, which in the P dialects tends to be narrowed in its pronunciation in varying extent from that of a French *û* to that of *î*. Thus, while Latin had *sus*, in English 'sow,' Umbrian had *sim* and *sif* corresponding to Latin *suem* and *sues* respectively, also *pir* and *frif* to the Greek πῦρ 'fire,' and the Latin *fruges* 'crops.' The first-mentioned word in Greek was ὗs, with an *u* more narrow than a French *ū*, and the French *ū* itself is one of the products of the same phonological tendencies of Gauls of the P group. I have already drawn your attention to the fact that such a Goidelic word as *cū*, 'hound,' is pronounced *cī* in the Brythonic dialects, and a strong tendency in the same direction is to be noticed in the case of other classes of words: take the Goidelic *tuath*, ' a tribe or a people,' which in North Wales becomes *tûd*, with a narrow *ū*, which in parts of South Wales becomes *î*. The tendency to make *qu* and *gu* into *p* and *b* respectively, and to narrow or unround the *ū* (sometimes also the *ŭ*), I should ascribe to the Neo-aryan invaders of the P group, but these inherited tendencies of their pronunciation spread themselves in very different proportions in the different lands seized by them. In Italy, not one of them was to any considerable extent imprinted on the language of the Q group, while in Greece it was otherwise. There *u* was regularly made into *v* with a decided inclination towards *i* which is the ordinary modern pronunciation, while only such dialects of ancient Greece as that of Crete, retained the long *u*. Similarly the labializing of *gu* and *ghu* into β and φ became the rule in Greek, though here and there the guttural held its own as in γυνή, genitive γυναικός, though not universally; witness Bœotian βανά, plural βανῆκες. On the other hand the *b* forms became the rule among the Celts of both groups, γυνή is in Goidelic ben ' woman,' English queen and quean. Without going into very troublesome details, one may say that the fusion of the dialects of the two groups was very considerable in the Hellenic world, while it was comparatively small in Italy.

Among the Celts it was far greater than in Italy, but not so great, perhaps, as among the Greeks. With regard to the mutual attitude of Gaulish and Celtican, we are without data; but as regards the British Isles, we have for our use the facts of Goidelic and Brythonic: the former has resisted the tendency of the P dialects to unround the $\bar{u}$ into $\bar{\imath}$, as well as to labialize the qu into p. On the other hand it has like the latter made gu into b, and there are other important points of similarity between Goidelic and Brythonic, which are to be accounted for by the influence of the latter. How then is this complication to be interpreted ethnologically? Geography comes to our aid to a certain extent: we have to suppose Aryans of the Q group in possession of most of the south of Britain, and to have extended their dominion sooner or later to the shore of the Irish Sea; then Aryans of the P group arrived and robbed them of portions of the south and east of their territory. Fresh arrivals of P Aryans would cause fresh encroachments on the Q Aryans, until at last the latter would be confined to tracts of the west, and even there they would probably come under the yoke of the conqueror. Thus we should have side by side a P language preserved on the whole free from the influence of the other language, and a Q language subjected more and more to the influence of the P language. Then hordes sail from the west to conquer Ireland, and they settle probably in Meath —I mean ancient Meath as approximately represented by the diocese of that name. Numerically speaking, they consist mainly of those whose language was the modified Q language alluded to. Thus there would be a people speaking that Q language in the western portion of Britain and in Meath in Ireland; but in the course of time the Q language this side of the Channel would give way wholly to the P language of the later Celtic comers. From that moment the only representative of that Q language would be the dialect transplanted to Meath and spread thence in the course of time to the whole of Ireland, and to Argyle, together with other parts of Britain.

This theory leaves the Goidels in the main nearly related to the ancient Romans, just as the striking similarity between Latin and Goidelic irrefragably prove; at the same time it makes the Goidel and the Brython inseparably related by reason of manifold race amalgamation, so that we are justified in speaking of the Neoceltic nations collectively as such, and not simply as Goidels and Brythons consisting of groups only distantly related with one another, which is the utmost one could have said of them before their fusion, as the case would also have been with the Romans and the Italians of the P group previous to the conquests of Rome and her sending forth her colonists to different parts of the peninsula.

The rise of the peoples of the Neo-aryan or P group within the Aryan world of prehistoric antiquity profoundly modified a portion of it, that is to say, what may be loosely termed its south-western half. Among other consequences it had probably that of driving the Q peoples further from their original point of dispersion, into Ireland and the corners of Gaul, into Spain, into Italy and Sicily, into Greece, into Asia Minor and possibly Armenia. The other half, so far as one can guess, was left unaffected, that is to say, the north-eastern half occupied by the Teutons, the Litu-Slaves, and the ancestors of the Aryan conquerors of Persia and Hindustan, who were probably helped to their homes in the East by the mighty current of the Volga and the waters of the Caspian Sea.

If I were asked to define more exactly what I mean by Q peoples and P peoples, I should say that the Q peoples who have occupied us in this lecture, the Goidels, the Latins, and the others in point, were simply Aryans, and all that is vaguely connoted by that term, just as in the case of the Teutons, the Slaves, and the Aryans of the East in so far as they are not merely Aryanized races of non-Aryan blood. On the other hand the Aryan of the P group is the ancient Aryan plus something else, in other words the term Aryan is here modified by an unknown quantity, which unknown quantity makes itself felt linguistically in such changes from original Aryan speech as have already been specified, together doubtless with many others which the glottological telescope, so to say, fails to make perceptible to us at this distance of time. What does this mean when translated into ethnology? I cannot exactly say, but one could hardly be far wrong in assuming it to imply a mixture of race, whatever else it may have involved. The Aryans conquered or assimilated and subdued another race in the neighbourhood of the Alps: the subject race learned the language of the conquerors while retaining its own inherited habits of pronunciation, and those habits of pronunciation in some cases prevailed and brought with them, among other things, the modifications of pronunciation which have occupied us in this lecture. Thus arose a modified form of Aryan language spoken by a Neo-aryan people of mixed origin, partly Aryan and partly something else. What race that other was I cannot say, and its physical characteristics would have to be collected to some extent from a study of the P peoples of this country, of Gaul, Italy, and other lands once possessed by them. Short of that it may be worth the while to mention that ethnologists seem to be fairly well agreed that the purely Aryan man had a long skull, whereas the builder of the Round Barrows of England was in the main a short-skulled man. Now those barrows were probably the work of the later Celtic comers, that is to say, of the Celts of the P group; so here at least a difference of bodily shape seems to combine with a modification of speech, to point to a difference of race between the P Aryans and the purer Aryans of the Q group.

It has already been suggested that this mixed race had its home somewhere in the region of the Alps, and one is tempted to ascribe to it the Alpine lake-dwellings which archæology has of late years been attempting to examine and reconstruct for the benefit of the student of prehistoric history, if I may venture so to call it. To illustrate the capacity of Alpine Europe, one has only to recall a few well known facts: consider for instance the southward advance of the Alpine Gauls, who seized on the rich lands of north Italy, and once on a time sacked Rome; think also of the Gauls who swarmed from the region of the Alps to overrun the East, and to plant the name Galatia in Asia Minor. Even in the time of Julius Cæsar we find the same sort of movements going on. Thus the whole people of the Helvetii leave their country to take forcible possession of another territory, namely that of the Santones in the west of Gaul. Had it not been for the interference of the Roman general, the Helvetii would have probably realized the ambition which they had so systematically cherished; and it is instructive to note that they were Celts of the P group, while the Santones, whom they were preparing to enslave, belonged probably to the older Celts of the Q group. This may be regarded as merely a late instance of movements which had often before originated in the region of the Alps.

JOHN RHYS.

TRACES OF A NON-ARYAN ELEMENT IN THE CELTIC FAMILY.

IN the previous lecture I spoke of the Celts as Aryans, but there is no doubt, that the Celts of modern times are also to some extent descended from non-Aryan peoples conquered and absorbed by the Aryan element. For there is no reason to suppose, that the Aryan settlers of the Celtic lands of history found those lands devoid of human inhabitants. Thus, besides the mixture probably inherent in the race of the P Aryans in the first instance, the Aryans of both groups may be supposed to have mixed to a certain extent with the aborigines; but one may expect this to have taken place in very different proportions. Thus the Q Celts, arriving first in these islands, would come in direct contact with the aborigines, and the later advent of the P Celts would, to a certain extent, drive the former Celts to make common cause with the ancient inhabitants against the invaders. In other words, the pressure of the P Celts may be presumed to have forced the Q Celts into closer relations, political, social, and domestic, with the earlier occupiers of the soil. What effect this may have had on the language of the Q Celts of the Continent, that is to say, on the Celticans, we have no means of ascertaining; but we are somewhat better off when we come to that of the Q Celts of the British Islands, since their language exists in the Goidelic dialects, which still offer themselves for comparison. Whatever may have been the extent of the modification undergone by Goidelic speech in Britain, there can be no serious doubt that, when it was transplanted to Ireland, it found itself in the midst of non-Aryan surroundings, which may have exercised considerable influence on it. On the other side the fact of the P Celts coming in the rear of the Q Celts makes it doubtful whether the P Celts ever came in contact in this country with the aborigines before they had been Goidelicized, excepting, perhaps, on their northern boundary, wherever the line was drawn between the Celts and the nation which survived in the North, as that of the Picts. Thus we may safely assume Welsh, Cornish, and Breton, to be freer from the influence of the non-Aryan element native to the British Isles than the Goidelic dialects can well have been. It is of importance to bear this in mind, since it is from a study of Goidelic that we are likely to obtain a faint glimmer of light on the pre-Celtic idioms of Ireland and the Pictland of the Scottish North. Let us, therefore, see how far this will help us.

One of the best defined things connected with Aryan speech is the system of personal names found to have been used by our Aryan ancestors. These names were usually compounds of more or less vague import, such as the Sanskrit Candrarâja, from candra, 'shining moon,' and 'râja, 'king,' or the Greek Διογένης, meaning a descendant of Zeus, Gaulish Πεννοουινδος from πεννος, 'head,' and ουινδος, 'white,' meaning white as to his head or white-headed, in Welsh *Penwyn*, and in Irish *Cennfhinn*, of the same signification. The number of words used as the stock elements of such compound or Full Names, as they have been technically called, appears to have never been very great among any Aryan nation; and there would seem to have been a tendency for the members of the same family sometimes to retain the same common element in their stock of names, as may be seen, for example, from such groups as Segimer, Segestes, Sigismund, and Segisdag, all occurring in the family of Arminius; or take the following, from the genealogies of the Welsh kings, Cadwaladr, son of Cadwallon, son of Cadvan, or Artgloys, son of Artbodgu, son of Bodgu. Another way of preserving an indication of relationship was sometimes practised still more economically, namely, by merely reversing the order of the elements of the compound as, for instance, in the case of an inscription from South Wales, which commemorates Vendubarr, son of Barrivend. This would be in Irish, Finnbhar, son of Barfhinn, and in Welsh, Gwynvar, son of Berwyn, or White-head, son of Head-white. A fashion of this kind is not quite extinct in Wales, where you may find that John Roberts is the son of Robert Jones, or Rowland Thomas the son of Thomas Rowlands. More instructive for our purpose, however, are the more exact parallels, such as the O. German Berhthari and Hariberht, which appears in English as Herbert, just as in the case of the Servian Dragomil and Milodrag, of the Sanskrit Devaçruta and çrutadeva, or of the Greek Θεόδωρος and Δωρόθεος. To say the least of it, these names cannot be said to yield the same sense, or an equally appropriate sense, when the order of the elements is changed, because, according to a rule of the Aryan languages, the prefixed word qualifies the one to which it is prefixed. Thus Θεόδωρος would have meant a god-gift, and according to the same rule Δωρόθεος should have meant a gift-god, which can scarcely have been the meaning of the compound as a man's name; it looks, therefore, as if the rule was in this case suspended, and the compound taken as a merely arbitrary joining of two words, much as we do with proper names still. Take for instance such a combination as Brown Robinson; that does not mean the Robinson with brown hair or the brown coat, but a Robinson who has a Brown in his pedigree, or whose godfather bore the name of Brown. In point of fact the reason may have been quite different, and of so arbitrary a nature as to be only known to Mr. B. Robinson's parents, uncles, and aunts. One of each set of the ancient compounds, such as Θεόδωρος, had doubtless a distinct signification, but its elements had their relative position reversed in order to make a new family name, while the question of the meaning of the new compound must have counted as of little consequence.

Lastly, the Full Names of this Aryan system were frequently cut down to one of their two elements, as for example in the case of names like the Sanskrit Deva-datta, 'god-given,' çiva-datta, 'çiva-given,' and the like, which gave rise to the shorter name Datta, or the Greek names of the group Νικόμαχος, Νικόστρατος, and similar ones, which have standing by their side the shorter forms Νικέας, Νικίας and Νίκων. In two of the Aryan languages, Latin and Lithuanian, Aryan Full Names are hardly known at all, having probably been superseded by shorter ones suggested by them. This, it must be confessed, is rather a hypothesis than a fact admitting of proof, though it is scarcely to be doubted that the Aryan Full Names must at one time have been normally represented in Latin and Lithuanian, both being languages which may be described as, in their later forms, much given to diminutival and hypocoristic forms. But the Celts retained the use of both kinds of nomenclature, the full names and the curtailed ones. I have already given instances of the former, and I need now only add, by way of giving a specimen of the latter, the name Catawc, in modern Welsh Cadog, as in that of the church called after the saint, Llan Gadog. This instance has the advantage, that we are told in the saint's life, that his baptismal name was not Catawc but Catmail, that is to say, in its later form Cadvael. This would have been in old Irish, Cathmál, and it meant a war-prince or battle-hero. It was a full name of the Aryan type, which had as its Welsh short form Catawc; but so far as we understand the relationship between these names, Catawc stood connected no more nearly with Catmail or Cadvael than with Cadwallon, Cadvan, or any other of the names beginning with the word *cat*, now *cad*, 'battle.' Similarly, to take an instance from the inscriptions of South Wales, the genitive Cunigni is the short name corresponding to full genitives like Cunocenni, Cunovali, Cunolipi, and the like, to which may be added Cunomagli, the antecedent of Conomagli. Cunign- is in later Irish Coinín, and in Welsh Cynin, as in the church name Llan Gynin, in Carmarthenshire. We have another short form of this series in Cunaci, now Cynog, as in Llan Gynog. So far as any rule can be made out as to the shorter forms, one may say that Cynin (Cunign-) and Cynog (Cunāc-) would be the forms suggested by names like Cunomagl-i and similar ones, while corresponding to Maglocun-i, we have Maelan (earlier stem *Maglagn-*) and Maelog. The exact relationship between these Full Names and their short correlatives is a subject on which more information is sadly wanting in the Celtic languages.

Enough, however, is known about both to enable us to identify traces of another and a very different kind of nomenclature in these Islands, a nomenclature which it will probably prove correct to regard as having come down from the non-Aryan aborigines. This is all the more worthy of notice as it belongs to the Goidels and not, excepting as a very rare case of imitation, to the Brythons.

The proper names in point are not compounds or even single words, but follow a formula, which, in some respects, reminds one of Semitic names like Abdastartus, 'servant of Astarte,' Abdiel, 'servant of God,' Obededom, 'servant of Edom,' and the like. Take for instance the Goidelic name Mog Néit, meaning slave of Néit, where Néit is found to have been the name of a war-god of the ancient Goidels. At any rate that is the tradition handed down in Cormac's Glossary, whose author, Cormac of Cashel, lived in the ninth century. Another name of this same formula was Mog Nuadat, which means the slave of Nuada. Now Nuada, genitive Nuadat, is known to be the Goidelic form of the god's name which was in Welsh Nûdd and Llûdd, while in the Roman inscriptions found among the ruins of his temple at Lydney on the Severn, his name assumes the form Nodens, genitive Nodentis. Here it is right to say that though the meaning of the name Nuada is unknown, it is found to have been common to Goidels and Brythons, and declined like a Celtic word. So in this instance, possibly, nothing can be supposed to be non-Celtic except the formula of the name, Mog Nuadat, or Slave of Nuada. There is another point to be noticed here, namely, that not only was Nuada the name of a god, but so also probably was that of Mog Nuadat. It might therefore be objected that this instance is of no avail for the study of the proper names of men. The fact, however, is that no line of distinction can be drawn between the names of men and those of their gods; and it happens that some of the most familiar names of men have also served as those of gods. Perhaps one should rather say that they were in the first instance names of gods which were afterwards appropriated by men. Take for example Toutiorix as a name of Apollo among the Gauls near the Rhine, and meaning probably the king of the tribe or the community. In Welsh it is represented by Tutri, Tudri, a man's name, and we have its counterpart in Teutonic as Theodoric, well known in modern High German as Dietrich, and in Anglo-Saxon as Theudric. In a word, such instances are so common that they suggest the larger question, whether the whole system of the compound names of the old Aryans was not first framed in reference to the gods and not their worshippers. Be that as it may, I come back to Mog Néit; and whether the first bearer of that name in Irish mythography should be regarded as a man or a god, we find the whole name (with its guttural silenced) in a form *Moneit*. Those who are familiar with the early history of this country will remember it as occurring in the Annals of Ulster, where they speak, under the year 729, of the engagement between Nechtan and Aengus. This has the additional interest of showing, so far as it goes, that the same peculiar system of proper names as in Ireland, obtained in this island, namely, among the Picts of Alban.

Other names of the same description are Mog Art, Mog Corb, Mog Lama, and Mog Ruith, in all of which Art, Corb, Roth, and Lama, may have been the names of divinities or some objects of reverence. This seems to have been especially the case with Corb, for besides Mog Corb or the Slave of Corb, one finds used as proper names such other instances as Fer Corb, 'Corb's Man,' Nia Corb, 'Corb's Champion,' besides more obscure ones such as Art Corb and Messin Corb.

Besides Nia Corb, already mentioned, we have a remarkable name, Nia Segamain, more correctly Nia Segamon or Champion of Segem; this, in its inscriptional form of Netta Segamonas, occurs on no less than three Ogmic monuments in the South of Ireland; and we know that Segamonas is the genitive corresponding to a Gaulish dative Segomoni used as one of the names of a Celtic god equated with the Mars of Latin theology. Thus by a name, Netta Segamonas, we are to understand one which meant the Champion of a Celtic Mars, called Segem. Other names like it appear in the Ogmic inscriptions of the South of Ireland, but they are more obscure, although they follow the same formula. The pedigrees, however, supply more instructive instances, such as Nia Febis, of which it may be here remarked that Febis is said to have been the mother of several remarkable characters in the epic stories of Erinn, namely, of the great druid or magician, Mog Ruith, of Lóch Mór, one of the most formidable of the antagonists of Cúchulainn, and of Echaid Mumo, usually regarded as the eponymous hero of Muma or Munster. Thus one cannot probably be far wrong in regarding Febis, from whom Nia Febis takes his name, as a goddess of the ancient Irish. Lastly, a name, Niad Fraich or Nad Fraoich, occurs; it is derived from the name of Fraech, a hero or divinity figuring in various Irish stories, especially that of the Táin, where his death at the hands of Cúchulainn is described. Fraech was the son of Buan, Queen of the Fairies, and a fairy host come and carry away Fraech's body with loud lamentation.

Another class of names was formed with the help of *fer* 'man,' such as Fer Corb, 'Corb's Man,' Fer Tlachtga and Fer Ceirtne. The first of these is based on the name of Corb, and the second on Tlachtga, the name of a daughter of Mog Ruith, and a goddess or heroine who has a considerable place in the legends of the Western Gael.

Another word of much the same import as mug or mog,' slave,' is *mael* (in Welsh *moel,* 'bald,') in such names as Mael-Patraic, 'the tonsured (man) of St. Patrick,' Latinized Calvus Patricii, and Anglicized Mulpatrick. A still more familiar name to you is Mael Coluim, 'the tonsured man of Columba,' Anglicized Malcolm. Add also Mael Muire, 'the tonsured man of the Virgin Mary,' sometimes Latinized Marianus. This class of names was not confined to males: witness such instances as Maelmedha and Mael Febhail, borne in the ninth century by women mentioned in the Four Masters' Annals of the Kingdom of Ireland. The best known examples of names of this formula seem to be Christian, but the formula itself is pagan, and probably ancient. Take for instance such a name as Mael Uma, borne by Baetan mac Cairill's son, who came over to this part of Britain to help Aidan and his Dalriad Scots, and to fight against the Angles of Northumbria. Mael Uma means 'the tonsured man of Uma,' where Uma literally means nothing but bronze, possibly bronze fashioned into a sword or spear. But whether one is to regard the bronze weapon as here personified, is not certain; for it was not unusual with the ancient Irish to personify their swords: we read that they swore by their swords and that their swords were supposed to contradict them in case of perjury. A more decisive instance perhaps as to the non-Christian origin of the formula is offered by a name Maelgenn given, in the story of Cormac mac Airt, to a druid contemporary with that Irish king. Cormac allowed himself to be converted to Christianity, at which the druid Mailgenn was so angry that he sent demons, so goes the story, to encompass the king's death, which they did by interfering to cause the bone of a salmon to stick in Cormac's throat so as to kill him. The druid's name Maelgenn appears to have meant 'the tonsured man of Genn,' a name which can be approximately identified. For we find three brothers Gann, Genan, and Sen-gan or old Gann, associated as leaders and kings of the mythic peoples of the Fir Bolg and Gailióin, whom Irish legend mixes up with the ancient inhabitants of Ireland. So one could scarcely err in regarding Genn as the name of one of the ancestors, probably reckoned divine, of the non-Celtic race in Erinn. In any case the fact of the name Mailgenn being borne by an Irish druid or magician hostile to Christianity, is fairly conclusive as to the formula of it having originated in pagan times, as well as among a non-Aryan race.

Other words were used in forming names of this kind, such as *céle*, 'companion or attendent,' as in Céle Petair, 'St. Peter's attendant'; and in this way was formed the term Céle Dé, 'Servus Dei,' which is Anglicized Culdee, and was once the name of a whole class of hermits: compare the Welsh meudwy, 'a hermit,' which literally meant also 'the slave of God,' and was very possibly first suggested as a translation of the Irish term. A still better known word in this respect is *gille*, 'a boy or attendant,' as in Gillechrist, 'servant of Christ,' Gillepatraic, 'servant of Patrick,' Gilleain, 'servant of John'; whence with *mac* prefixed comes the name Maclean, and Gillefinnen, whence similarly Maclennan. It is needless to add other instances, and I will only mention that, under the influence of Irish Christianity, a few names were formed by the Brythons after the Irish pattern, such as Gwas Dwyw, 'God's Slave,' Gwas Sanffrêd, ' St. Bride's Slave,' Gwas Teilo, 'St. Teilo's Slave,' and Gwas Patric, 'St. Patrick's Slave.' This last became historical in Strathclyde and well-known in the form of Quospatric and Gospatrick, also written Cospatrick. Of the relations of the earl Gospatrick with William the Conqueror and with the Scotch king, Simeon of Durham speaks at some length, and how Gospatrick finally stood on the Scotch side is well-known. Perhaps as compared with the other names which have been mentioned, those formed with the word *gille* are to be considered comparatively late: hitherto I have not lighted upon one which could be said to be for certain of pagan origin.

The formula of these names one and all, if non-Aryan, as I believe it to be, goes to prove a fusion of an Aryan race with another people existing formerly in Ireland, and probably also in the north of this island, especially those parts occupied by the Picts. In fact such names were to be found at home more especially among the Picts. Take for example that of Macbeth, Maelbeth, and Maelcon. The Norse sagas which speak of the affairs of North Britain, know nothing of Duncan; but they speak of Karl Hundason, or Churl Hound's Son, in whom we seem to have a reference to Macbeth, with Beth rendered *hund*, ' a hound.' That this conjecture is worth considering follows from another fact: when Cnut came to the North, three princes made homage to him, namely, Malcolm; a certain Jehmarc, whose name, evidently corrupt, has been identified by Dr. Skene with Imergi borne by one of the chiefs of the Isles, and à certain Maelbaethe, whose name in its more usual spelling would be Maelbeth. For this name occurs elsewhere, borne, for example, by an Irish abbot of Devenish in Lough Erne, whose death is given by the Four Masters under the year 944. Nor was king Macbeth the first Pict alluded to by that name in this country; for the Norse sagas mention a Magbiodr fighting with the earl Sigurd, and long before that we read in the Saxon Chronicle of an Irish pilgrim of the name

Maccbethu paying a visit to the English king Alfred. So both Macbeth and Maelbeth were real names current both in Ireland and in the land of the northern Picts. Now it has been argued that the Maelbeth who did homage to Cnut must have been no other than the Macbeth who became king of Scotland; for St. Berchan gives Macbeth thirty years of power, which, reckoned backwards from the date of Malcolm's accession in 1058, carry us back near the time when a mormaer of Murray died in the year 1029. Then Macbeth may have been already in power, so that the Maelbeth who did homage to Cnut may be argued to have been Macbeth.

But when it is further suggested that the name Maelbeth was an error for that of Macbeth, the source of the error is left unexplained to an extent it need perhaps not be; for it is possible to take another view of it, namely, as in the case of the name Mog Nuadat or 'the Slave of Nuada.' Now Mog Nuadat is the common form of that name in Irish literature, but we know from Cormac's Glossary that the name was in full, and in what may be presumed to have been a more original form, Mog Mac Nuadat or 'the Slave Son (or Boy) of Nuada.' Similarly I should suggest that the Pictish prince was called in full Mael Mac Beth 'the tonsured man Son of Beth,' and that this name, Mael Mac Beth was shortened sometimes into Maelbeth and sometimes into Macbeth. So it would scarcely be right to say, that there was any error there to be explained away. That is not all, for this conjecture accounts satisfactorily for the Norse name, Karl Hundason, where *karl*, meaning 'a churl or common man,' just renders *mael* as the Irish for a tonsured man or a servant. If I am right in treating Beth as the equivalent of the dog or hound of the Norse Hunda-son, we may be said to be here on the track of an ancient totem of the non-Celtic peoples of these islands. But Macbeth and Maelbeth would have to be regarded as containing a non-Celtic word retained untranslated; when fully translated into Goidelic they appear, according to the view here advocated, as Mac Con and Mael Con, Hound's Son and Hound's Slave respectively. The latter name, Mael Con, figures more than once in the background of the history of the

Northern Picts, for their powerful monarch in the time of St. Columba was Brude Mac Maelchon, called by Bæda, *Bridius filius Meilochon*, and some two centuries later another Brude Mac Maelchon, who, opposed to Aengus, was conquered by him in the year 752. As to Mac Con, a personage of that name figures largely in Irish mythography, being made, among other things, to pass a part of his time in Britain and to die in Munster. This Mac Con may perhaps be regarded as one of the mythic ancestors or representatives of the non-Celtic race here in question.

This sort of name cannot be dismissed without directing attention to a considerable class of Irish names in which the bearer of each is styled a hound. The best known, perhaps, is that of the hero Cúchulainn, which means the Hound of Culann the Smith: both names, Cúchulainn and Culann, may be perhaps unhistoric, but that does not touch the historical character of the names; they appear from the beginning of the 6th century down. Take, for example, Cú Ulad, 'Hound of the Ultonians,' lord of Uachtar-thire in the present County of Down, who died in 1061; Cú Cuailgne, 'Hound of Cuailgne,' who in 1011 kills the chief of Conaille, including the district called Cuailgne or Cooley, as its name is pronounced in English; Cú Corb, mentioned in connection with a battle supposed to have taken place in 506; and Cú Coigcriche, 'Hound of the Frontier'; Anglicized Cucogry, the name of a distinguished historian of the 17th century, who was one of the so-called Four Masters. A trace of a Christian use of *cú*, much in the same sense probably as *mael* or *gille*, seems to occur in the name Colman Canis, known only in this Latin form in Adamnan's *Life of St. Columba*. In Irish it would possibly have been Cú Cholmán. But, as in the other instances, there can be no doubt that the formula was a pagan one. It occurs, in fact, on an inscribed cromlech in Kerry, where one reads in ancient Ogam, Conu-Nett maqi Conu-Ri, which put into the nominative would be, in modern Irish, Cú-Néit mac Con-Ri, that is to say, Néit's Hound son of Ri's Hound. The spot is near the high mountain now called Caher Conree, that is to say, Cathair Con Ri or the Arx of Cú Ri, where Cú Ri is the name of a mythic personage filling a great place in Irish legend, and more commonly called Cú Roi mac Daire in modern Irish.

The Dalriad Scots used the same sort of names, as will be seen by a glance at the early history of Scotland, where such instances occur as the following: Cú cen Mathair, 'Hound without a Mother,' the name of one of the sons of Echaid Buide, son of Aidan. This name, strange as it sounds, was well known in Ireland, and borne, for instance, by a king of Munster said to have died in 664. A man called Cú Bretan, son of Congus, is mentioned dying in the year 740; his father, Congus, was probably the same Congus whose kindred struggled against the power of Aengus and the Men of Fortrenn. Cú Bretan meant seemingly the Hound of the Brythons in the sense, presumably, of one fighting against them, though the contrary would seem to be the case with regard to Cú Ulad, 'Hound of the Ultonians,' and Cú Caratt, 'Hound of the Friend or Kinsman,' in both of which and many others the idea seems to have been that the man was to be the champion and defender of those whose hound his name described him to be. Another of the names here in point was Cú Cuaran, in Latin Canis Cuaran, king of Picts and Ultonians, whose obit is to be found under the year 706. Cú Cuaran means Cuaran's Hound, as to which one has to add that Cuaran occurs as the name of a Munster saint, called Cuaran the Wise, but whether Cú Cuaran was so called after a saint or not, the name meant Cuaran's Hound, and accordingly the well-known name of Anlaf Cuaran meant Cuaran's Anlaf, but why Constantine's son-in-law and ally against Æthelstán should have been so designated is not recorded.

Besides these names with cú, 'hound,' the word Cuilen, 'whelp,' is found to have been not unknown as a royal name in Alban, as for instance in the case of the king, called Cuilen, son of Indulph, in the 10th century; it was a common name also in Ireland. But more interest attaches to a name Macmisi, for Fergus Mór mac Erc is said to have been otherwise called Macmisi Mór, where Macmisi is to be analysed into *Mac Mise* or 'the Son of Mes,' and the latter word occurs in the

Irish, mess-chú, which is explained to mean a lap-dog or a pet dog. Here, however, cú is probably employed as originally explanatory of *mes* which occurs in a proper name, Messbuachallo, which would seem to have meant Shepherd's Dog, though it designated the mother of Conaire Mór, a king of Tara, famous in Irish legend. His name, Conaire, is also derived from *cú*, 'hound,' genitive *con*, though in what sense it is impossible to say, whether as resembling a hound or as having to do with hounds: in this last respect nothing is known except that he owned a famous dog: compare the Welsh name Cynyr of the father of Kei or Cai, Arthur's butler. In any case, the Irish myth makes Conaire son of Messbuachallo and of a father named Edersceol of the race of Ier or the Erna of Munster, that is to say of the non-Aryan race of the south-western portion of Ireland; and the whole story is a remarkable instance of the native element making its influence perceptible in the legends of that country. Further, a name Mes Corb is found borne by the eponymus of a clan located in the hills of Wicklow, and calling itself Dál Mes Corb, or Dal Messin Corb, the Division or Sept of Mes Corb. The latter's name, as meaning Corb's Dog, is to be compared with the other Corb names, such as Fer Corb, Nia Corb, Art Corb, Mog Corb, but more especially Cú Corb or Corb's Hound.

Lastly, there is another curious name somewhat of the same type as Cuilen, 'whelp,' but the interest attaching to it is far greater: I allude to the name Moddan, which is probably to be explained as meaning a dog or whelp, and of the same origin as the Irish word madadh, 'dog.' In the history of Scotland, the best known bearer of the name was perhaps Moddan, Karl Hundason's brother or brother-in-law, who was defeated in the war with Thorfinn and slain by Thorfinn's general, Thorkell Fostri. This Moddan is doubtless the name which some of the Sagas have rendered Hundi, which may be explained as a derivative (formed after the fashion of Norse names) from the word hund, 'hound or dog.' Further, Hundi Earl was the name also given by the Norsemen to a chief who fought with Sigurd the Stout, earl of Orkney, in a previous age. It may also be mentioned here that more than one

Norseman of mixed descent in the Orkneys is alluded to under the name of Hundi or of Hwelpr, that is to say, 'Catulus or whelp.' As you all know, a Saint Modan is mentioned by Sir Walter Scott in his Lay of the Last Minstrel, where the words run thus :—

> 'Some to St. Modan pay their vows,
> Some to St. Mary of the Lowes.'

It is perpetuated in Ireland in the name of Kilmodan Abbey, in County Longford; and the ancient genitive of the name occurs in an Ogmic inscription at a place called Windgap, in the north of the County of Waterford: it is there written Moddagni, and the man so-called belonged to one of a people designated Mocu Luguni, whose name appears in various parts of the south and west of Ireland. Before dismissing this name, I must call your attention to what may probably be regarded as a dialectic variation of it, taking the form Muadhan: it was borne by a character figuring in the epic story of Diarmait and Grainne. We read as follows:— 'Diarmuid and Grainne rose early on the morrow, and journeyed straight westward until they reached the marshy moor of Finnliath, and they met a youth upon the moor, and the feature and form of that youth were good. . . . Diarmuid greeted that youth, and asked tidings of him. "I am a young warrior, seeking a lord," quoth he, "and Muadhan is my name." "What wilt thou do for me, O youth?" said Diarmuid. "I will do thee service by day, and I will watch thee by night," said Muadhan. Then they made bonds of compact and agreement one with the other, and journeyed forth westward—I ought to have said that Diarmuid and Grainne were all this time fleeing from one place to another before Finn Mac Cumhail and his Fiann—until they reached the Carrthach; and when they had reached that stream, Muadhan asked Diarmuid and Grainne to go on his back, so that he might bear them across over the stream. "That were a great burden for thee," said Grainne. Then he nevertheless . . . bore them over across the stream.' We have a long account of Muadhan's services to Diarmuid and Grainne, including his carrying Grainne for a mile or two every now and then when she was tired of walking; but the part of his doings I wish particularly to direct your attention to is the following: one day when Finn's men were on the heels of Diarmuid, a venomous hound of the most formidable description was let loose on the fugitives. On that occasion Diarmuid's big servant asked the former to walk with Grainne whilst he, Muadhan, warded off the bloodhound. The story proceeds thus:—'Then Muadhan went back and took a hound's whelp from beneath his girdle, and set him on the palm of his own hand, and when this whelp saw the pursuing hound rushing towards him with his jaws and throat open, he rose from Muadhan's palm and sprang into the gullet of the hound, so that he reached the heart and rent it out through his side; then he sprang back again upon Muadhan's palm, leaving the hound dead on the plain.' Not long afterwards, Muadhan takes his leave of Diarmuid much against the latter's will, and it is to be noticed that the district here in question extended from Dunkerron Mountains south-west of Killarney to Limerick and the Shannon: here Diarmuid as a hero of the west was at home. The big man who offers him his best services may probably be regarded as in some way representing the Ivernian and native population of Munster, and the invincible little dog which he carried about on his person may be taken as the form given in this story to one of the principal totems of the race.

While I am on this question of totems, I should like to lead you back to an incident in the story of Cúchulainn's death. Before the hero of an Irish epic tale succumbs to his fate, he is made to violate his *gessa* or break his taboos: this happens in the case of Cúchulainn, for, as he hies forth against his foes on the fatal day, he is asked on his way to turn aside and partake of food which is cooked by three one-eyed hags; it was moreover dog's flesh. He resisted for some time, for it was one of Cúchulainn's *gessa*, we are told, not to eat of the flesh of his namesake; at last he gave way, but it was with the result that the usual strength abode no longer in his arm, or even in the side of the body which had touched the meat.

The way in which Cúchulainn's objection to partaking of dog's flesh is expressed in the story suggests, that the idea was not wholly unfamiliar in ancient Erinn, that some mysterious connection existed between the human namesake and the animal whose name he bore.

The prominence given to proper names involving an apparent reference to the dog is to be accounted for, in part perhaps, by the fact that the word was used in a very wide sense, as the Goidel has been in the habit of calling the wolf, the fox and the otter, each a dog; that is respectively wild dog, red dog, and water dog. With regard to the otter, it may be mentioned that the names of the nobles of Buchan in the *Book of Deir* contain among them not only a Mac Bead, Bede the Pict, Matáin, and Matadin the Judge, all of which are here in point, but also the name of a man described as son of Mac Dobarchon, whose name means 'Son of the Water-dog or Otter'; and one would perhaps not be far wrong in supposing, that we have water-dog left untranslated and, probably, to some extent inaccurately written in the strange looking name of Usconbuts in the *Pictish Chronicle*, where it is said to have been borne by one of the early Pictish kings. As to the fox, it had, of course, other names beside that of red dog, such as *sinnach*, which appeared occasionally in Irish nomenclature, where such names may be instanced as O'Sinaich and O'Sinacháin; and fox also was the meaning of the name Loarn, whence Cenél Loairn or the Race of Loarn, one of the three branches of the Dalriad Scots, so called from an ancestor Loarn Mór, or the Great Fox. This totemistic name gives its designation to the marquisate of Lorne at the present day. In North Wales an ancient inscription occurs dating probably from the fifth or sixth century, and giving a name of this kind, translated into Latin as *Filius Lovernii*, 'Son of the Fox Man.'

Let us return for a moment to the wolf, which besides being called some kind of dog, such as the wild dog or the dog of the woods, had also the peculiar appellation of Mac Tire, meaning literally the Son or the Child of the Land, which would seem to imply that the wolf was once regarded as the aboriginal inhabitant, the veritable autochthon of the country. If this should seem not sufficiently to the point, let me call attention to what Giraldus says of the descendants of the Faelchú or wolf of Leinster: they were to be found in Ossory, that is, approximately, the modern counties of Kilkenny and the neighbouring portion of Ormond or East Munster. Giraldus Cambrensis relates a story about one of these human wolves meeting a priest in a wood and begging of him to administer the sacrament to her, which he did after hearing her account of herself. In return for his kindness she prophesied to him of the coming of the English to conquer Ireland. But a more interesting account occurs in the Irish version of Nennius, where the wolf-people of Ossory rank as the fourteenth wonder of Ireland. The passage freely translated reads thus: 'There are certain people in Erinn, to wit, the race of the Leinster Wolf in Ossory, who pass into the forms of wolves [literally sons of the land] whenever they please, and kill cattle according to the manner of wolves, and they quit their own forms. When they go forth in the dog-forms they charge their friends not to remove their bodies, for if they are moved they will not be able to come again into their bodies; and, if they are wounded while abroad, the same wounds will be on their bodies at home, and the raw flesh devoured by them while abroad will be found in their teeth.' That is the Irish account of the descendants of the Leinster Wolf, and the anthropologist will readily recognize in it two orders of ideas. In the first place the going out of the men from their bodies is a part of the ancient idea of dreams, according to which the soul issued from the body and actually visited all the scenes which the dreamer seemed to visit, and it has been a matter of caution among savages in all ages not to move or wake a person thought to be dreaming, lest the soul should not find its way back into the body. That this view was acted upon in ancient Ireland can be proved from Irish literature. But that the soul, when it went forth from the body, should have the form of a wolf, is quite another matter, and seems to me to point to a survival of the totemistic idea as to those descendants of the Wolf of Leinster.*

---

* The subject of lycanthropy is too large to be discussed here, but the reader may be referred to Clodd's *Myths and Dreams*, pp. 81, etc.

These facts pointing to ancient totems I should refer to a non-Aryan source, as there is no good evidence of totemism to be extracted from our Aryan data, though I have little doubt that the Aryans once had their totems also; but it was earlier, and the whole scheme had, as such, been blurred and obliterated some time anterior to that which can be reached by Aryan philology. However, this is only an inference, and the case as to a non-Aryan race in these islands must rest much more on the proper names, which yield us very definite non-Aryan formulæ. These, together with other indications of a like nature, go to make up a case against the notion that the Aryans formed the first and only human inhabitants of this country in early times; so the Celts of the present day represent in various degrees the two elements amalgamated, the Aryan conquering caste, and the non-Ayran aboriginal owners of the soil.

JOHN RHYS.

THE MYTHOGRAPHICAL TREATMENT OF CELTIC ETHNOLOGY.

WITH the aid of proper names I attempted in the previous lecture to shew that the British Isles had once a population which was, in point of origin, other than Celtic and Aryan. It is now time to look what Celtic mythography has to teach us on this question of race; and as the stories in point cluster thickest around Erinn, it is convenient to begin with the Sister Island, and listen to what she has to fable about the settlements and divisions of the country between the ancient inhabitants. For ancient Ireland, the mother country of the Scot, is the key to Alban, his later Scotland in Britain.

Now, Irish legend not uncommonly divides Ireland into two halves, a northern and a southern half; they are named Leth Chuirn, or Conn's Half, and Leth Moga, or Mog's Half, the person meant in the latter case being Mog Nuadat, otherwise known as Eogan Mór, whence some of his reputed descendants were termed Eoganacht or Euganians. This division of Ireland into halves is not to be regarded as a fact: it has none of the characteristics of a real boundary between warlike peoples, and I suspect that primarily it was one between Connaught and Munster; for one can hardly be wrong in treating Conn's Half as synonymous with Connacht, the native form of the name of Connaught, which is derived from that of Conn, and may be loosely rendered Conn's people or Conn's descendants, just as if you called the

Campbells collectively the Campbellry, or the Macphersons the Parsonry, and so in other cases like that of the Eoganacht already mentioned. There is, however, no denying that Irish legend-mongers have usually applied this process of bisection to Ireland as a whole. It was embodied also in a story with quite other names, to wit those of the sons of Míl. This latter story in one of its simplest forms derives the peoples of Ireland from two brothers, sons of Galam or Míl, that is to say the Warrior, and those two brothers who so curiously recall Romulus and Remus, sons of Mars, were called Emer and Erem. So one of the oldest specimens of Irish literature, namely, Fiacc's Hymn, describes the whole population of Ireland as consisting, before St. Patrick's mission, of *meicc Emir, meicc Erimon*, 'the sons of Emer and the sons of Erem.' The descent from the two sons of Míl takes us back to the so-called Milesian invasion; but the division between the brothers is seldom spoken of in the territorial sense, as in the case of Leth Chuinn and Leth Moga.

The mythographers pretend, however, that Emer, the eldest brother, took the southern half of Ireland, and Erem, the younger, took the northern. But Erem, like Romulus, slew his brother and took possession of the whole island, which reads like an epitome of the history of Celtic conquest in Ireland; for Erem, genitive Erimon, means a ploughman or farmer, and the bearer of it was, in point of name at any rate, a sort of western Aryaman and Aryan invader, who slays Emer, the representative or eponymus of the aborigines. The name Emer, written also Eber, is disguised after the fashion of old Irish spelling in which every vowel-flanked *m* and *b* were pronounced like *v* or approximately so: thus you will perceive how *Emer* is really closely akin with the name of the ancient Ivernians of the country, and how it covers the historical fact, that in the two kingdoms of Munster, as the Erna of Munster, they last retained their nationality and their hostility to the encroaching Aryan. At best, the division of Ireland into two halves was of the very roughest kind; and when one wished to make any approach to accuracy it was necessary to make qualifications and reservations. The first consolidated conquests made by the Celts in Ireland consisted probably of what they called Mide or Meath, in allusion to its central position: roughly speaking, it was the district represented by the bishopric of Meath or by the counties of Meath, Westmeath, and Dublin.

At a later stage, the Aryans probably made further conquests from Meath as their basis of operations: thus among others they extended their dominion into Ulster at a time which the chroniclers give as 331 A.D., and acquired the territory called Airgialla or Oriel, that is to say, all the south of Ulster as far as Lough Neagh, the Newry River, and Carlingford Lough. The ancient Ultonians dispossessed were pushed beyond this boundary into the north-east corner of Ireland, consisting of the present counties of Down and Antrim. To distinguish the retreating Ultonians from the Ultonians in the more indefinite acceptation of the word, the former are called True Ultonians, which the victorious Ultonians of Oriel, being Celts, were not. Besides Ultonians, they are also called Ulidians, the Old Irish name being Ulaid in the nominative case and Ultu in the accusative. Now these Ulidians or True Ultonians could not be reckoned descendants of Erem, who was the Aryan ancestor, nor could they very conveniently be associated with Emer, who was wont to be connected with the southern half of the island: so they are found treated as the offspring of an ancestor called Ir or Er, who is made out to have been another son of Míl. The fact, however, is that Ir and Emer are forms of one and the same name Iver or Ever, for according to the usual rule of Irish phonology, a *v* flanked by vowels disappears wholly, so that Ever becomes in Irish Er, and Iver becomes Ier and Iar. But owing to some peculiarity of dialect in Munster the *v* sometimes remains, and is written *m* or *b* in Old Irish not only in Emer or Eber but also in the genitive Duibne of the name of Diarmait O'Duibne's ancestress: we have inscriptional evidence that Duibne was Dovinia, so that had *Duibne* followed the general rule it ought to show no *b* or any other consonant representing the *v*. Thus it turns out on examination that the legend, however manipulated in later times, makes for the common descent of the Ivernians of the south-west and the Ulidians of the north-east from one and the same son of Míl. This is not a mere matter of inference, since Emer is found also called Ier, Er and Ir, as in the pedigree of Conaire Mór, where Ier is said to have been one of the Erna: he was in fact the eponymus of the Erna, whose name put back into its early form would be Ivernii or Evernii. This brings us near to the form given in a reference to Ireland in Adamnan's Life of St. Columba as it reads in the oldest manuscript, namely, that which dates from the beginning of the eighth century: the words in point are *in tua Evernili patria;* also to the name of Ireland as occurring in the Itinerary of Antoninus, written *Iverio*. It is a mention, which has mostly been overlooked, made of an *Insula Clota in Iverione*. Now Clota we know from other sources as a name of the river Clyde, and the island of that name was probably either Arran or Bute in the Firth of the Clyde; and it is much after the manner of Ptolemy to treat the islands on the west of Britain as belonging to Ireland, which Ptolemy did, for example, in the case of the Isle of Man, and even of Anglesey. The name Clota becomes in Welsh Clûd, which in Welsh literature is so treated as to lead one to think that it was a name belonging to Celtic mythology. In the first instance, it may be presumed that the river and the island were associated with Clota, as a divinity to whom they were once considered sacred, or with whom ancient paganism had in some way connected them. In the mediæval Welsh romances called the Mabinogion, a remarkable character called Gwawl son of Clûd figures as a solar hero: his name means light, and he is overcome by being rashly induced to step into a little bag in which he suddenly disappears, reminding one of the ancient Greek notion of the sun descending in its western course into a golden bowl. In *Iverio, Iverione*, it is to be noticed that we have probably a Brythonic form of the name rather than a Goidelic one, as the latter would have been declined somewhat differently, making Iverio, genitive Iverennos, or the like.

However, we can trace the name into a nearer connection with Scotland, namely in the late form Erann, which in Irish literature does service as the genitive plural of Erna, when the Munster people of that name are spoken of: thus we read of their ancient capital as Temair Erand, 'Tara of the Erna or the Ivernians,' which lay somewhere near Castle Island in Kerry. Now this name Erann or Erand appears in the middle of Scotland, however it came there: I allude especially to Sraith Hirend as the Goidelic representative of Strathearn, and to such phrases as *for bruinnibh Eirenn*, 'on the banks of Earn,' which show that the name was that of the river and of the loch, just as it was of a river Erne in the north-west of Ireland and of a loch in the same neighbourhood; but was it as native in Alban as it was in Ireland? that is a question which I would rather leave alone for the present. Such Greek forms of the name of Ireland as Ἰέρνη are as modern in point of phonology as the latest Irish forms, and in this respect the Welsh Iwerddon and the Latin Iberna or Iuberna, as given in some manuscripts of Juvenal, are much more valuable; but all the Latin ones come down from a time when Latin *b* might also have the value of *v*. However, a graffito to be seen till lately in the Palace of the Cæsars in Rome is said to have read Iverna; and the reading Juberna* is not the best which the manuscripts of Juvenal and Pliny afford, as some of the former give Iuuerna, which the editors, as might be expected, treat as *Juverna*, to be further murdered in some scholars' mouths into *Jewverna*. But the spelling Iuuerna represents not *Juverna* but *Ivverna* or *Iwwerna*, which is placed beyond doubt by the early spelling found in the oldest Ogam inscriptions of Ireland and Wales. It is needless to say that it cannot be a mere accident that this unclassical spelling should have found its way into a manuscript of Juvenal. But the Ogmic doubling of the *v*, whatever it meant, was optional, so that Iverna must also count as a good form, and we have the *v* duly rendered by ov in Ptolemy's Ἰούερνοι or Ἰουέρνιοι, 'the Erna,' and Ἰουερνίς, the name of a town in Ireland. The Latin of Irish authors, with the exception of the *Evernilis*, to which allusion has been made, usually gives us the forms with *b*: thus the Confession of St. Patrick has *Yberiones* for the people of Ireland, and *Yberionacum* as a form of the adjective, which is now *Erionnach* in the sense of 'Irländisch, or belonging to Ireland.' As to the meaning and etymology of such a name as Iverio, I may mention that I once suggested that it stood originally for Piverio, to be explained

---

* According to Lewis and Short, this is one of Pomponius Mela's forms of the name, but Frick in his edition, iii. 6, gives only *Iuverna*.

as of the same etymology as the Sanskrit *pīvan*, Greek πίων, which make in the feminine *pīvarī*, πίειρα, 'fat,' or 'plump': thus Erinn would seem to mean the fat or fertile country, and this suggestion has found acceptance at the hands of no less distinguished a Celtic scholar than the Leipsic professor, Dr. Windisch. The Celts are known to drop original *p*, and my etymology is, so far as I know, phonologically admissible, but you must understand that this is no proof of its soundness: it only means that no objection to it can be raised on the score of the analogy of other words: it supplies no direct proof that it is the right account of the word. On the whole, I have been myself obliged to give it up, for two reasons: there is no proof that the word is of Celtic origin, but rather the contrary, as it reminds one of such a national name of a non-Aryan people as the Iberi of ancient Spain and Gaul; and in the next place there is no certainty that we have here to set out from the name of a country rather than from that of its people, which makes a considerable difference. For though the conjecture, that Iverio or Erinn meant the Fat Country, should pass unchallenged, we should have, on the other supposition, to regard it as deriving its name from a race which was styled, by itself or by its neighbours, the Fat Men. This is for various reasons which you can readily supply for yourselves, not highly probable; but it is nevertheless what we should have to believe if we regarded *Ever*, for instance, as etymologically prior to Iverio and Erinn. It will be seen later that this priority is not improbable; and on the whole I am disposed to regard all these names as non-Celtic words, the original meaning of which is unknown.

The first settlements of Ireland figuring in Irish literature are those associated with the names of Partholon and Nemed. The latter's name is to be found also in Welsh literature, and it is probably Celtic, as the story is both Celtic and Aryan. The story of Partholon is a duplicate of it, being, as I am inclined to think, roughly speaking, that of Nemed subjected to the modifying influences of a native Ivernian medium. This is countenanced by the fact that Partholon's settlement in Ireland is placed before that of Nemed, and more especially by the name Partholon itself being utterly obscure in point of meaning and characterized by an initial *p*, which makes it impossible to regard it as originally Goidelic. Moreover Partholon is made the descendant of an ancestor called Srú, son of Esrú, and the former of these names is attested by a genitive *Srusa* in an Ogam inscription in the west of Kerry. Everything in fact goes to shew that the name of Partholon comes from the Ivernians. But, modified slightly, the name is well-known to you in this country as that of the Clan Pharlane, or Macfarlanes. The clan belongs, I learn, to the Highland district of the earldom of Lennox, and it is supposed to be so called from a certain Parlan, whose name is explained as another form of Bartholomew. The manuscripts of Nennius give the name of the Irish Partholon as Partholomæus and Bartholomæus it is true, but that is probably an instance of a superficial process of translating proper names, of which you in Scotland are not quite without instances: whence come your Hectors? have they nothing to do with the common Goidelic name Eochaidh? and has not the name Dermot, through the medium of the form Diarmait and a palatal pronunciation of the dentals, been known to be properly Anglicized as Jeremy, to the delight, no doubt, of the dreamers engaged in the task of finding the Ten Lost Tribes of Israel? Against the charter evidence, said to prove the descent of the Clan Pharlane from Parlan, grandson of Gilchrist, son of Alain, Earl of Lennox, I have nothing to say; but it does not help us to account satisfactorily for the introduction of the ancient name Parlan, and the conjecture I would offer is, that Parlan or Partholon had figured from time immemorial in the family legend of the Gaelic Earls of Lennox as a great ancestor, and possibly as a divine personage. The eventual appropriation of the name of the divine ancestor by individuals claiming descent from him has its parallel in the fate of many names of gods. In fact, the descent of the names of divinities to human namesakes is not very different in its nature from the descent of royal names from the throne to the gutter, as illustrated by the rising crop of little Victorias now said to adorn the slums of London.

The legendary account of the Milesian conquest of Ireland tells us that the island was at the time of that event under the sway of three princes, whose wives left their names to the country, whence it may be inferred that the latter were goddesses associated with Ireland, or, perhaps, personifications of the Island or of certain parts of it. One of the three husbands is associated with Usnech in Meath, and is called Mac Greine or Son of the Sun, and the name of his wife was Eire or Erinn, which is still the name of the country. That she was supposed to have a personal existence some time or other, is proved by the Welsh equivalent Iwerydd occurring both as the name of a woman and previously as that of a goddess, the mother of Brân, and inferentially wife of Llyr, god of the sea. Another of the three Irish princes of the legend was Mac Cuill, whose name is of uncertain interpretation, and whose wife was called Banba, associated with Slieve Mish in Kerry; but Banba is one of the poetic names for Ireland, and what is more curious still is, that it is the ordinary name for a part of Alban, namely Banff in the heart of the Pictish country of antiquity, not to mention a well-known Bamff* in Perthshire. The remaining Irish prince in point was called Mac Cecht which has usually been supposed to mean the Son of the Plough, and is found associated with a spot in Tipperary; his lady's name was Fodla, which is also a poetic name for Ireland; nor is that all, for we find it likewise in Pictish Alban, namely in the name of Athole, which in Goidelic was written Ath Fodla, supposed to be correctly rendered into English as Fodla's Ford. Whether that be so or not, the mythographers of this country in enumerating the sons of the ancestral Cruithne or Pict, call one of them Fodla or Fotla, and treat him as giving its name to Athole. There was a fourth name of Ireland which the Irish historian Keating wished to regard as even older than the foregoing; it was Elga, which he interpreted as meaning noble. Curiously enough a nearly allied form of what seems the same name meets us in the Pictish part also of Alban, namely in the name Elgin, which is spoken of about the end of the 13th century as Castrum de Elgyn, and possibly the name of Glenelg in the west involves the same vocable. Now the appearance of these names and such names as these in the Pictish parts of this island, and in that

---

* Sir James Ramsay of Bamff House, in that locality, reminds me of the existence likewise of a Bamff Well near Coupar-Angus.

portion of Irish mythology which treats of the præ-Celtic story of Ireland is very remarkable, and the theory of their having all been imported into Britain from the Sister Island is hardly to be entertained. I am, therefore, inclined to regard the names in question as belonging, in virtue of a common speech and a common origin, to the non-Celtic aborigines of both islands.

Allusion has been made to Fodla as a son of Cruithne the eponymous hero of the Picts; but it may be further mentioned that Cruithne has in all seven sons ascribed to him to account by means of their names for the seven provinces of which the Pictish kingdom, north of the Forth, was anciently regarded as consisting. One list of these provinces is supposed to date from a time when the kingdom of the Dalriad Scots was independent of the Pictish power, and here the names offer no difficulty; for they are (1) Angus and Mearn, that is the counties approximately of Forfar and Kincardine, (2) Athole and Gowrie or Perthshire, except most of the portion of that country lying west and south of the Tay, (3) Strathearn and Menteith or the south-western portion of Perthshire, already mentioned; (4) Fife and Fothreve, or the counties of Fife and Kinross; (5) Marr and Buchan, or the counties of Banff and Aberdeen; (6) Moray and Ross, or the counties of Elgin, Nairn, Inverness, Ross, and Cromarty; and (7) Cathanesia, on both sides of the mountains. Here you see the number seven was rather traditional than real, as all the provinces are subdivided; but in the case of Cruithne's sons the number meant was undoubtedly seven, and the list may reasonably be supposed earlier than the one I have already given, for two out of the seven are subject to some uncertainty as to their identity. A quatrain ascribed to Columba gives the names thus :—

> Seven sons there were to Cruithne,
> Seven parts they made of Albany,
> Cait, Ce, Cirig, martial men,
> Fib and Fidach, Fotla, Fortrenn.

The arrangement is alliterative, as one must see at a glance; and of the seven, Cait connects himself with Caithness, Cirig with Mag Girginn, that is to say, Mearn, meaning the Plain of Girg or Girec, Fib with Fife, Fotla with Ath Fotla or Athole, and

Fortrenn with the district of that name, including Strathearn. This leaves two to be placed, namely, Ce and Fidach, who between them must be supposed to represent the Marr and Buchan, and the Moray and Ross of the other scheme; but which did Ce represent and which did Fidach? Possibly one would not greatly err in regarding Glen Fiddich in Banff as echoing the name of Fidach. In that case one might treat Fidach as the representative of the Marr and Buchan of the other list, and it would remain simply to connect Ce with the Moray and Ross of the same.

This conjecture derives confirmation from a careful interpretation of the passage in Adamnan's Life of St. Columba, where St. Columba is represented sojourning in the island of Skye. There he receives a sudden visit from two young men, who arrive in a boat, bringing with them their aged father to be baptized by the saint, but the latter can only preach to him by interpreter, though he is said to have been the chief of the *Geona Cohors*. This remarkable term cannot but suggest the question, what *cohors* can have meant in such a context, for it is not likely to have referred here to a purely military organization, but rather to one that was tribal, or, more correctly speaking, both tribal and military at the same time. This application of the word *cohors* is probably to be compared with Pausanias using the term ἡ Γενουνία Μοῖρα in speaking of a people of Britain in the early days of the Roman occupation. I must explain that these Genunians are represented by Pausanias as Roman tributaries invaded by the powerful tribe of the Brigantes, who thereby bring on themselves an attack at the hands of the Romans. The Brigantes occupied the country now represented by the North of England and a certain area this side of the border, while the Genunians must have been neighbours of theirs, who required to be protected against them. The nature of the feud between them is unknown, but it probably arose in part at least, from a difference of race; for the Brigantes were Brythons while the Genunians were very probably the non-Brythonic ancestors of the people known sometimes as the Picts of Galloway, and identical probably with the

Niduarian Picts of Bede. These terms *cohors* and μοῖρα remind me of nothing tribal among Brythonic peoples, but it is not hard to guess what Goidelic term they were both meant to render: unless I am greatly mistaken it was dál, which meant a part, portion or division, the etymological equivalent in fact of the English *dole*, German *theil*. *Dál* itself was very possibly but the literal rendering of a Pictish or Ivernian word which occupied the ground before the triumph of Goidelic among the aboriginal race: at any rate it occurs often enough in the tribe-names of Ireland, such as the Dál Fiatach, Dál Riada and Dál n-Araide, the *n* of which shows that the noun dál was a neuter. That is to say, when pronounced in full, at a time when the language still retained its Aryan case-endings, it was dālŏn or dālăn. In *Dál n-Araide* we have the nasal of the neuter retained after the vowel of the ending has been silenced: this remnant of an earlier stage is usually detected very plainly when the succeeding word begins, as it does here, with a vowel; for before a consonant assimilation takes place and Dālŏn Ceon, which I take to have been the antecedent of the form of the name rendered *Geona Cohors* by Adamnan, must become Dālŏc Ceon. Then a further change takes place making the *cc* into *g* according to the common habit of Goidelic speech. Thus when the vowel of the case-ending goes out Dālŏc Ceon- (for Dālŏn Ceon-) survives as Dál Geon.

The form Geon, however, has no existence as such except under the influence of the neuter dál or words like it, and as soon as it assumes an independent place it should also resume the radical form Ceon; but my conjecture is, that this was overlooked in the manuscripts of Adamnan's Life of St. Columba, and that the reading *Geonæ Cohortis*, due in them to the influence of some such a form as Dál Geon, is less correct than if it had been written *Ceonæ Cohortis*. This interpretation of the term has the advantage of giving a local habitation and a name to a tribe to whom it is thus found possible to assign Cruithne's son Ce as their eponymous hero. This people, ignorant of St. Columba's Goidelic speech, dwelt probably on the mainland, somewhere opposite Skye as the representatives of the dominant race of Picts of which King Brude mac Maelchon was the powerful head at the time of St. Columba's mission. This is favoured by the name of the old chief baptized by Columba, for it was Artbranan, which is presumably the same as the Irish *Art-bran*, and to be compared with that of *Art-Corb* mentioned in the previous lecture: neither name, so far as I know, occurs in the nomenclature of the Brythonic Celts. Lastly, it may be worth while mentioning that it is owing perhaps to the prevalence of names like Dál Ge or Dál Geon in the Western Highlands that the Norsemen gave that part of Scotland the designation of Dalar, which it bears in their literature.

It is not my intention in this lecture to try to discuss the names Scot and Pict; and it is needless to tell you that the former is not found confined to Scotland in the modern sense of that term: nay, the original Scotland was Ireland or a part of it. In Latin authors, Scottus is usually employed as the equivalent for the word Goidel, which it is important to bear in mind, without in any way attempting to equate these words either as to origin or original signification. The similarity of sound between Scottus and Scythes or Scytha, 'a Scythian,' has led the legend-mongers into all kinds of extravagance about the eastern origin of the Scotti and their wanderings in quest of Erinn. However, one item of some value seems to lie concealed beneath their heaps of rubbish, as it implies a native story which they did not entirely invent. They make Míl, the ancestor of the Milesian conquerors of Erinn, marry a daughter of Pharaoh, king of Egypt: she is called by them Scotta, whence the Scotti are made to derive their national name. The Milesians, including among them Scotta, land in the south-west of Ireland, and the lady's death in the story is associated with a spot in Kerry between Slieve Mish and the sea. Of course, the mention of Scotta, daughter of Pharaoh, required as its complement a very detailed account how the Goidels got into Egypt, and how they came from there through Spain to Kerry. That, however, need not detain us, and the question for us is rather how the legend-mongers came to postulate the existence of Scotta. In the first place, it was probably a name which they found already in existence, and belonging to the same class as Eire, Banba, Fodla and Elga: it was, I take it, countenanced or perhaps even suggested by the name of some people in Ireland. As to making

Scotta out to be a daughter of Pharaoh, the latter name is doubtless based on the superficial resemblance of a native name to the biblical Pharao, genitive Pharaonis, as it occurs in the Vulgate. Such a native name is by no means hard to find: in fact, the difficulty is rather that more than one such seems to satisfy the conditions. Perhaps the most probable is that of a certain Fearon, said, according to one legend, to have been one of the four sons of Partholon, who divided Erinn between them as follows:—Er took the country from Ailech Néit in the north as far as Dublin; Orba the country from Dublin to the island of Barrymore, near Cork; Fearon from Barrymore to Clarin Bridge in Galway; and Feorgna from there to Ailech Néit in the north. So Fearon, whose name is the one here in question, has the very district in the south-west with which the legend associates the name of Scotta. Another legend makes Ær, Orba, Fergna and Feron, sons not of Partholon but of Emer, and all connected with Munster. This differs from the other, but that matters little; for whether you make Fearon son of Emer or son of Partholon, you make him an Ivernian, and one is thereby encouraged in supposing the name Scot derived from Ivernian origin too.

Just as *Scottus* did duty as the Latin for *Goidel* or Gael, so *Pictus* or Pict was used in Latin as the equivalent of the name Cruithne. Thus the kingdom of the Northern Picts, already mentioned as consisting of seven provinces, was termed in Goidelic Cruithen-tuath, the community of the Cruithni or Picts, and in Latin as Pictavia 'Pictland.' Besides this it has usually been supposed that there was, as already suggested, a Pictish people on the Solway between the Esk and Loch Ryan, but it is not so generally known that there were Cruithni or Picts in various parts of Ireland, as may be gathered from occasional allusions to them in Irish literature. Thus the epic story of the Táin Bó Cuailgne speaks of Maive, queen of Connaught, marching to devastate the Ultonians and the Cruithni, and in this connection it mentions Slieve Gulann, more usually called Slieve Gullin, in the present county of Armagh, and alludes to Maive storming Dun Severick, in the neighbourhood of the Giant's Causeway. It is implied that one of these localities, possibly both, were in the territory of the Cruithni. In fact this would be the country afterwards inhabited by the people driven out of Oriel by the Celtic conquests of the Three Collas in 331, the tribes already mentioned as the True Ultonians or Ulidians, and called also the Clan of Conall Cernach. The territory which they retained east of the Newry River and Lough Neagh kept the name of Ulad or Ulidia, while the people themselves of the more southern portion of that district were known specially as Cruithni and Dál n-Araide (Latinized Dalaradia), so called from an ancestor, Fiacha Araide. Their country may be said to have consisted of the County of Down and of Antrim as far as Glenarm. Beyond them, and extending as far as the mouth of the Bann, were the closely allied people called the Dál Riada. They were probably meant to be included among the Cruithni or Picts of the epic story of the Táin, but in historical allusions to them the Dalaradians are usually called Picts, and the Dalriads are called Goidels or Scotti. Both peoples, driven to the north-east corner of the island, sent forth swarms to Britain; and the outcome, in the case, for instance, of the Dalriads, was the Scottic kingdom of Argyle.

What, then, was the distinction between these peoples that one tribe should be called Cruithni or Picts, and the other Goidels or Scots? It was probably one of language, and possibly of religion; the Dalriad Scots were Christians, and they probably spoke Goidelic, while the Dalaradian Picts may have been still using their native Pictish or Ivernian speech; and they remained Pagans probably later than the Scots. What other differences there may have been prominent between them it is impossible to say; but all Irish history goes to shew that they were closely kindred communities of Cruithni, and I take it that the names Cruithni and Scots may have been originally applicable to both alike. Now the term Scot, though probably one of the ancient names of the aborigines of Ireland, hardly ever occurs in Irish literature; but in its Latin form of Scottus it is used to translate Goidel or Gael, and this possibly gives us the kernel of the distinction between the Scots of Ireland and the Cruithni or Picts of that country: the Scots were Cruithni who had adopted the Celtic language of the Aryan conqueror in Ireland, a people in fact that gloried in being Goidels and endeavoured to forget their Cruithnian origin. In other words, they were disposed to imitate the Aryan in their speech, in their religion, and in their institutions to the extent, for example, of giving up the so-called Pictish succession through the mother, though this continued late among the Christian Picts of North Britain. To the Brythons of antiquity Ireland was a country divided between two races, the Goidelic and the Scottic: the Goidel they spoke of by that name, as it is still in its Welsh form of Gwyddel, my countrymen's word for an Irishman. They must have also had the other word; for it was through the Brythons of South Britain that the names of the more remote peoples of these islands seem to have reached the writers of antiquity; but while the Brython might go on speaking of the non-Aryan native of Ireland who paid unwelcome visits to this country as a Scot, that Scot by and by learned a Celtic language, and insisted on being treated as a Celt, as a Goidel, in fact: that is, I take it, how *Scottus* became the word used to translate Goidel.

Let me now return for a moment to the Cruithni of Ireland, and some of the allusions to them. Among the first may be mentioned the Picts opposed to St. David in the south-west corner of Wales. Their leader was a certain Boia, whose place of abode has a name still extant at St. David's, namely, Clegyr *Vwya*. He and his people were pagans, and they may naturally be supposed to have come from some part of the south of Ireland: the name Boia seems to a certainty to connect the man so-called or his race with the Boi of the story of Cairbre Musc and his son Corc in Munster, to whom I have called attention in my Hibbert Lectures on Celtic Heathendom. In the next place may be mentioned a reference by Adamnan to a priest whom he calls *Pictus*, and whose charge he places somewhere in Leinster: it was presumably among men of his own race. But be that as it may, we are expressly told that he was Cruithnian or Pictish. Nay, there were Picts in Meath as late as the 7th century, for Tigernach, the father of Irish chroniclers, gives under the year 666 the obit of Eochaid Iarlaith, king of the Cruithni of Meath. Whether this prince was himself one of the Cruithni, or a Celt of the ruling class of the Goidels does not appear, and it is remarkable that while he is called king of the Cruithni of Meath, his name, Iarlaith, meant either Ivernian prince or else prince of Ivernians. That can hardly be a mere accident, and one is tempted to draw the conclusion that the title 'king of the Cruithni of Meath' was only introduced as a sort of explanation of the designation Iarlaith,* whence it would follow that the *Iar* of the compound Iarlaith functioned here at one time as a synonym of *Cruithni*, and the antecedent of the *Ever* already mentioned. Such allusions as these, which careful reading would doubtless enable one largely to increase in number, go to shew that even in the most Celtic portions of Ireland the ancient inhabitants formed little islands, distinguished by the use of their ancestral speech and inherited paganism, while Celtic influence and Celtic culture had effaced them in the surrounding districts. It is natural, however, to suppose that the last thing to distinguish the Cruithni from those around them may have been a servile tenure of the soil to which they were attached.

In Connaught and Munster one should perhaps consider Celtic influence as having been comparatively late in leavening the Ivernian mass; and here the story of one of the colonizations of Ireland is worth mentioning: it is given in the Life of St. Cadroe, supposed to have been written in the tenth century. The immigrants arrive from the direction of Spain, as usual, and land somewhere in the west of Ireland: they take possession of Cloyne on the river Shannon, and find the country inhabited by the race of the Picts: *gentem Pictaneorum reperiunt.* Here may also be mentioned a tract on the servile tribes of Erinn in the fifteenth century Irish codex, known as the *Book of Ballymote:* besides assigning to the Picts a part of Ulad and a locality which has not yet been identified, it places some of them in the north and some in the south of what is now the county of Roscommon. It also describes the more northernly Picts as extending from the Shannon to Lough Foyle, and from the neighbourhood of Donegal to the river Bann.

---

* The Angles ruling over the Picts of Galloway seem to have given their sons names exactly parallel; witness Pect-helm, the name of the bishop of Whithern and Bede's friend.

The name Pict appears to have been native in Scotland, and its treatment as synonymous with Cruithne has already been pointed out, while the inclusion of the Cruithni of Ireland in this synonymity is an important fact proving, that the peoples so designated were formerly held to be identical in habits and language to a greater or less extent, whether they were found in Britain or in Ireland. This is on the whole countenanced by Gildas in what he has chosen to tell us in his usual fashion of straining after effect. He speaks of Picts and Scots as differing from one another only in part, *moribus ex parte dissidentes*, while they agreed in several points which he has been pleased in his own way to mention, namely, the same avidity to shed blood, the same hairyness of face, the same truculence of countenance, and the same shameless habit of wearing no breeches. This is the evidence of a Brython full of the sincerest hatred for both Pict and Scot. Happily such bitterness of race in this island has long since died out. I need look for no remoter proof or pleasanter to me than the fact of my standing before you, and the indulgence with which I have thus far been heard by this intelligent audience, consisting, as it does, of the descendants not only of Brythons, but of Picts and Scots, of Norsemen and Angles alike.

JOHN RHYS.

THE PEOPLES OF ANCIENT SCOTLAND.

IN this lecture it is proposed to make an attempt to understand the position of the chief peoples beyond the Forth at the dawn of the history of this country, and to follow that down sketchily to the organization of the kingdom of Alban. This last part of the task is not undertaken for its own sake, or for the sake of writing on the history of Scotland, which has been so ably handled by Dr. Skene and other historians, of whom you are justly proud, but for the sake of obtaining a comprehensive view of the facts which that history offers as the means of elucidating the previous state of things. The initial difficulty is to discover just a few fixed points for our triangulation so to say. This is especially hard to do on the ground of history, so I would try first the geography of the country; and here we obtain as our data the situation of the river Clyde and the Firth of Forth, then that of the Grampian Mountains and the Mounth or the high lands, extending across the country from Ben Nevis towards Aberdeen. Coming now more to historical data, one may mention, as a fairly well-defined fact, the position of the Roman vallum between the Firth of Forth and the Clyde, coinciding probably with the line of forts erected there by Agricola in the year 81; and it is probably the construction of this vallum that is to be understood by the statements relative to Severus building a wall across the island. In the next place may be mentioned as fairly certain that Ptolemy's Dumnonii extended from the coast of Ayrshire and the Firth of Clyde across the rivers Clyde and Forth to the vicinity of the Earn, two of the towns which he ascribes to them being situated beyond the Forth, namely, Alauna, supposed to be at Ardoch, or somewhere nearer to the Allan; and Victoria, further on in the direction of the Tay. Add to this that there can be no reasonable doubt that the Dumnonii were a Brythonic people of the P group, like the Welsh, the Cornish, and the Bretons, as well as the ancient Gauls, and not a Goidelic people of the Q group, like the Goidels of Erinn, Man, and Scotland. To be more accurate, let us only say that the ruling classes among the Dumnonii were Brythonic, leaving the descent of the bulk of the people a matter of uncertainty. Then, lastly, there remains, from a previous attempt of mine to fix a few points in this early history, the indubitable fact of the virtual identity of the name of the Verturiones of Ammianus Marcellinus with that of the province of Fortrenn, which approximately consisted of Menteith and Strathearn.

The extensive tract of country, whose boundaries are sufficiently indicated by a mention of the Roman Rampart, the Grampians and the Mounth, is a fairly well-defined one, and it proved the theatre, so to say, of the principal acts in the history of the kingdom of Alban. Now, of the seven eponymous sons of Cruithne mentioned in a previous lecture, three have their local habitation and their name in this region, to wit, Fortrenn, Fib, whose name echoes that of Fife, and Circinn, whose name forms part of that of the Mearns in its Goidelic form of Mag Circinn, the Plain of Circinn or Girg. Without the qualification introduced by the word *mag*, 'a plain or field,' *Circinn* may be interpreted territorially to have meant the tract consisting of Angus and the Mearns. At any rate this agrees with the 12th century tract, enumerating the provinces as the result of dividing Scotland between seven brothers, the sons, doubtless, of Cruithne; but in the tract each province is sub-divided, and Circinn gives place to *Enegus cum Moerne*. Similarly, instead of Fib we have *Fif cum Fothreve*, which, by thus supplementing Fife, extended the province to the vicinity of Stirling, the Ochils, and Abernethy. The treatment of Fortrenn is the same, except that the name Fortrenn disappears, to wit, in favour of *Stradeern cum Meneted*. The same tract also gives a list of the seven provinces or kingdoms, as it calls them, without reference to the seven brothers but by defining them mostly according to their geographical boundaries. In the Cisgrampian region which concerns us now, this latter list, like the previous one, places three realms: the first is an inland tract from the Forth to the Tay, evidently including Fortrenn; the second begins from Athran, that is to say Athrie, near Stirling, and takes in the bends of the coast as far as Hilef, supposed to be the river Isla; but the Liff has also been suggested, which flows into the Tay where Perthshire and Forfarshire meet on the Firth of Tay. In either case, therefore, this kingdom would comprise not only *Fif cum Fothreve* but also possibly a part of Gowrie. The third kingdom in this region extended from the Hilef to the Dee, so that it took in *Enegus cum Moerne* or the modern counties of Forfar and Kincardine. Putting aside the subdivision it will be seen that these arrangements agree in dividing Cisgrampian Alban into three regions, but that they show a difference real or apparent with regard to the north-eastern boundary of the middle realm.

If you will for a moment turn to Ptolemy's Geography, you will find that he assigned only two peoples to this Cisgrampian country, namely, the Dumnonii, whose northern territories came within it, and another people called the Vernicones, to whom he gives only one town, namely, Orrea, which is perhaps to be sought somewhere near the confluence of the Orr or Ore Water with the Leven in Fifeshire; but the territory of the Vernicones must have extended north towards the mountains as Ptolemy makes it conterminous with the land of the Vacomagi to the north-east of the Dumnonii. It is this dominion of the Vernicones with Gowrie carved partly out of it, and partly perhaps out of the land of the Dumnonii, that seems to have yielded the two provinces of Fif cum Fothreve, and Enegus cum Moerne. It will have been noticed that the Vernicones in Ptolemy's Geography contrast very strikingly, as possessed of only a single town, with the Dumnonii who had no less than six, and they may be presumed to have been of a different race. This is countenanced by the fact that neither Orr nor Fife seems to be a word of Celtic origin. There is some difficulty about the exact form of the name of the Vernicones in the manuscripts of Ptolemy, but assuming *Vernicones* to be the correct one, it would have to be regarded, it seems to me, as a name given them by their Brythonic neighbours: in modern Welsh it would sound *Gwern-gwn*, and mean the 'Hounds of the Marshes,' or 'Marsh-dogs.' In that case it may be supposed to have had reference to the dog totem of some of the non-Aryan aborigines, and to imply by antithesis that there were other dog-peoples known to the Celts of Britain, which is not improbable, as I have already tried to show.

As to the relative position of the Vernicones, the fact of the whole of the Cisgrampian region being represented by the Brythonic people of the Dumnonii under various names, such as Mæatæ and Verturiones, goes to show that the Vernicones were overshadowed by them: in fact the latter may be supposed to have been for a time at any rate reduced to the position of a subject race, regarded either as a sort of a client state dependent on the Mæatæ, or else ruled by adventurers gone forth from among the Mæatæ to make conquests of their own among their non-Aryan neighbours. It is important, however, to bear in mind that the Vernicones seem to have, as a people, remained non-Celtic until they came under the influence of Goidelic institutions and language, and it is especially necessary to remember this antagonism of race between Brython and Vernicon, when one comes to consider the difficult question, how the central region about the Tay came to be Goidelic. Ptolemy wrote about the year 125 A.D., from information dated probably some years earlier; but one may contrast the number of his tribes with the appearance at the opening of the third century of the same tribes under two names alone for the whole of the North, namely, Mæatæ and Caledonii. Here the single name of the Mæatæ takes the place of the two names of Ptolemy's northern Dumnonii and the Vernicones. The Mæatæ were threatening the Roman province we are told, and the Caledonii were preparing to help them in spite, as it is said, of promises made by them to the contrary. In the Mæatæ we have in all probability the leading people of Cisgrampian Alban—the Verturiones of Ammianus—and their clients or allies. For Dio Cassius, abridged by Xiphilinus, gives his readers to understand, that they were tribes who lived in the district adjoining the Roman Rampart, and that they inhabited the plains and marshes of the country.

This describes, with some approach to precision, the home of the northern Dumnonii, if you include that of the Pictish peoples overshadowed by them. As to the Caledonii, we are told that they lived beyond the Mæatæ, a description which, while it requires no comment, suggests one good reason why they, in this instance, followed the lead of the Mæatæ; but the latter were probably more advanced in the art of war, for the reason, if for no other, that their land bordered on the Roman province, and their name seems to claim for them the attribute of boldness and daring *par excellence*: it has the appearance of being a Brythonic word of the same origin as the Welsh word *meiddio*, 'to dare.'* At any rate, it is with them and not with the Caledonii that the Roman governor, Virius Lupus, had to treat; for failing to obtain the reinforcements which he wanted, he had to purchase peace at a great price from the Mæatæ. A few years later the natives of the North brought upon themselves the great campaign of Severus in 208, one of the results of which was that they had to give up a considerable tract of country to be garrisoned by Roman soldiers. It was probably the country between the Clyde-Forth Rampart and the river Tay. This is supposed to be attested by the remains of strong stations, which historians are inclined to ascribe to the Romans—one, for instance, at Fortingall, not far from where the Tay issues from the lake of the same name; another at Fendoch, on the Almond, where that river emerges from the Grampians; and a third at Ardoch, where the remains in question are, as I am told, to be distinguished from what has sometimes been taken for Agricola's camp.

In fact, we learn from Tacitus' account of the campaign, which Agricola undertook in the year 80 in the region beyond the Forth, that he afterwards had forts, *castella*, built in it, and that after his victory over Calgacus in the year

---

* Or shall we connect it rather with the Welsh *maedd-u*, 'to beat'?

86, he returned through the country of the Boresti, where he received hostages. This introduces a name, Boresti, otherwise unknown, but the bearers of it were probably a portion of the Dumnonii, or some people subject to them between the Tay and the Forth. Much the same peoples may be supposed to have given hostages, and allowed *castella* to be built in their midst both by Agricola and Severus. These structures of the Roman army seem to have formed in the eyes of the Northerners such a remarkable feature of the district that they gave rise to a new name for it. At any rate, the designation, Verturiones, under which the Mæatæ appear later, admits of being best explained with reference to these military works. This name Verturiones appears first in the pages of Ammianus Marcellinus, referring to the events of the year 364, in which the northern inhabitants of Britain made a determined attack on the Roman Province. Their onslaught was for a time stemmed by the arrival of Theodosius in 369, and one of the results of his victories in the North was that he caused the *castella* of Agricola and Severus to be re-occupied as a protection against the future inroads of the tribes beyond the province. At any rate, this would seem to be a fair inference from the words of Claudian, when he glorifies Theodosius as—

' Ille Caledoniis posuit qui castra pruinis.'

Be that as it may, the inhabitants of the North, collectively and loosely called Picts, without any regard to the Celts among them, were then divided into two nations, as we are told, namely, the Dicalydonæ and the Verturiones. In the former race we have a collective term meant to include all the mountaineers, while the latter has its echo in the later Fortrenn, the inhabitants of which could not all be called Picts, except in a sort of geographical sense; and the name Verturiones was probably in the main geographical, if we may judge from the use of Fortrenn as the name of a district, with its Brythonic people usually called Fir Fortrenn or Men of Fortrenn. But the term Mæatæ had not been forgotten in Adamnan's time, as he calls them by the slightly modified forms Miati and Miathi in his life of St. Columba written in the last decade of the seventh century and preserved in a manuscript which is not later than the early part of the eighth. Adamnan there speaks *de bello Miatorum* which Aidan king of the Dalriad Scots was carrying on, and about whose success St. Columba was very anxious. This particular engagement, fought in the year 596, has been identified with a battle known otherwise as Cath Circinn or the Battle of Circinn. This tends to shew that it was fought in the district for which Circinn, son of Cruithne, was invented as the eponymus, the district otherwise described as the kingdom of *Enegus cum Moerne*. Very possibly it was Aidan that first gave Gowrie its individual existence, namely, by clearing it of the Mæatæ, that is to say the Brythonic Men of Fortrenn. In any case, the allusion to the Battle of Circinn in the course of Aidan's war with the Mæatæ forms the first hint admitting of being construed into evidence of a Goidelo-Scottic people having penetrated into the heart of the Cisgrampian region. Lastly, it falls so readily to its place here, that I cannot help regarding it as the first recorded event in the series of fierce conflicts of which the history of a later age gives us glimpses from time to time, as Brython and Scot return to the struggle for supremacy on the banks of the Tay.

The Brythons, known as Mæatæ and Verturiones or Men of Fortrenn continued on the whole to have the best of it down to the time of Kenneth macAlpin; for previous to his reign and the triumph under him in 844 of the Gaelic speaking population, the kingship of the southern Picts was in the power of the Men of Fortrenn for rather more than a century, beginning with the ascendency of Angus son of Fergus, in 731, over Goidels and Picts. Throughout that period the Men of Fortrenn had constantly to maintain their sway by force of arms, so that finally when they had received a crushing defeat from the Danes in 839, Kenneth macAlpin was able in a short time firmly to establish himself and his Scots in power. This was the end of the rule of Fortrenn, but it is evident, that, from the dawn of northern history down to that time, the Men of Fortrenn, whether as such or as Verturiones and Mæatæ, had with a few short interruptions been the most formidable people in the Cisgrampian area. They were either lords of the greater part of it or at any rate they were more powerful in the long run than any other people within it. They were of sufficient account for Agricola to have castella built in their country, and for Ptolemy a little later to ascribe several towns to them as northern Dumnonii, while Dio gives them as Mæatæ the lead of the Caledonii in their attacks on the Roman province in 201 and the succeeding years. Ammianus mentions them as Verturiones, taking an active part against the Province in 364; and towards the end of the sixth century as the Miati of Adamnan they are engaged in a war with antagonists consisting probably both of Scots and Picts likewise, and it is some such a combination that was destined ultimately to overcome them. Nevertheless with some intervals in the time between St. Columba and the triumph of Angus son of Fergus, their power sufficed to carry the rule of Fortrenn down almost to the middle of the ninth century; and during far the greater part of the seven centuries and more following the campaigns of Agricola in Britain, Cismontane Alban virtually meant the Brythons of Fortrenn. They had, however, a formidable foe before the Scots were settled on the Tay, and that was the Pict or Caledonian who held the strong position of Dunkeld and other posts on that river. On the whole, however, the introduction of a Goidelo-Scottic people to the Tay Valley, is, in my opinion, to be interpreted as an admission on the part of the Pict that he was unable single-handed to withstand the advance of the Brython: in other words the Scot was called in to render aid to the Pict before it occurred to the Scot to fight for his own hand.

Thus far the Brythons have mainly occupied us: let us now turn our attention to the other peoples of North Britain which Tacitus calls Caledonia. That name alone raises the presumption that the Caledonians were at one time the most important people there; but one of the great difficulties of this question is that their name has for some reason or other been nowhere retained in modern Scotland with the single exception perhaps of Dunkeld,* which means the *dún* or fortress of the Caledonians. Further, the geography of Ptolemy has difficulties of its own, when one comes to examine his account of the northern half of Britain. Among other things, his Scotland, instead of running north is turned round towards the east, so that what should have been its western coast forms its northern side, and that its eastern coast looks towards the south. Moreover his Ireland as a whole is placed too far north, so that his Scotland, had it occupied its proper place, would have overlapped a part of his map of Ireland. The most probable explanation is, that he had before him three maps without meridians or parallels of latitude, a map of Southern Britain, a map of Northern Britain and a map of Ireland. The map of Southern Britain reached north as far as the Wear and the Solway, for that is the latitude at which he goes wrong. As to his map of Ireland, it is necessary to point out that its north-east corner seems to include several of the islands which are wont to be reckoned with Britain, together with parts of what may be suspected to have been corners of the mainland of Britain. A mistake of this kind appears also in the Itinerary of Antoninus, when it places the island called Clota in Iverio, that is to say in Ireland. Now that I have warned you of this error, which one has to bear in mind when making use of Ptolemy's geography, I may proceed to what he had to say of the various tribes of Caledonia.

Next to the Dumnonii and in a north-westerly direction from them, he places a people whom he calls Epidii, and he terms the Mull of Cantyre the Epidian Promontory. Add to this that an island apears on the north coast of Ireland called Epidium, which is very possibly the Mull of Cantyre detached in manipulating the three maps. This suggestion, made by Mr. Henry Bradley, is countenanced by the fact that to the north-west of it is placed another island called Malleus, which, judging from its name, may be presumed to have meant that

---

* It is right to say that Mr. Macbain would give us a second instance in the latter part of the name of the Perthshire mountain, Schiehallion, the Gaelic for which he gives as Sith-Chaillinn.

of Mull. These are two out of a group of five islands to which the geographer gives in common the name Æbudæ, and of the remaining three two have no other name than that of Æbudæ, which may be guessed to have been Islay and Jura. The fifth of the group is given the name Rhicina; and this may have really belonged to Ireland; its name suggests that of Rathlin, called in Irish Reachrainn. It does not appear whether one should suppose the name Αἰβοῦδαι to be in any way related to that of Ἐπίδιον. Beyond the Epidians—and probably beyond Loch Linnhe—Ptolemy places in succession along the coast tribes bearing the names respectively of Cerones, Creones, Carnonacæ, Cæreni and Cornavii. These last were at the extremity of the island, and appear to have been so called from one of its headlands likened to a horn, the word for horn being in Welsh and Irish *corn*. This form of the name was Celtic, and Southern Britain had a people between the Dee and the Mersey called the Cornavii, and there are such other traces of the name as that which survives in the modern name of Cornwall; but which headland the Northern Cornavii were called after by Ptolemy's Celtic informants one cannot tell; for the north-west and the north-east corners would do equally well.

So there are here several points of great uncertainty in the geographer's precarious outline. Thus nobody knows how far towards the north of the island he supposed the Epidii to extend. We are therefore at liberty to say that it may have been right up to the northern boundary of the present county of Argyle, for ancient landmarks are apt to persist. So one makes a guess at the same time at the southern boundary of the Cerones, but one is no better off with regard to the northern frontier of their land. Some help, however, seems offered by the modern topography, as we may perhaps venture to regard the name of the Cerones as echoed by the modern Carron. In that case it might be concluded that Loch Carron opposite Skye was in the country belonging to the Cerones, and that the latter extended to Glen Carron and the head of Dornoch Firth, into which the Carron Water flows. Along the west coast it may have extended to Loch Broom, or possibly as far as the southern boundary of the present county of Sutherland. You will notice, however, that this crowds the other three tribes, the Creones, Carnonacæ, and Cærini together on the west coast of Sutherland. In other words, they would have to be considered as very small communities; but a very different explanation is possible, namely, that two or all of these three names may have been merely variant readings of a single name. I wish, however, to leave that question for a moment in order to return to it from the other side.

After disposing of the western coast the geographer begins anew from the country of the Dumnonii, by saying that the Caledonians extended from the Lemannonian Gulf to the Estuary of the Varar. The former would seem to have been a gulf taking its name from the same source as the district called *Levenach* and Anglicized *Lennox*; so the gulf may have been Loch Long or Loch Fyne, or even Loch Lomond, erroneously regarded as a part of the sea. As to the Varar, that seems to be exactly what is now Farrar, the name of the river which near its mouth is called the Beauly. Above the Caledonians, according to Ptolemy, lay the Caledonian Forest, that is to say, probably to the west of them, and between them and the tribes bordering on the west coast, while to the north of the Caledonians comes a people called Decantæ, and beyond them the Lugi, who bordered on the Cornavii. Above the Lugi, that is to say, more inland, he places a people called the Smertæ, and this completes his map of the tribes on that side of the Caledonians. Here our uncertainty is left a narrower range than on the west coast; still it is considerable; for, though the Caledonians extended to the Estuary of the Varar, as the nearest point touched by them on the seaboard in that direction, they may have extended a good deal further north and east; in fact it is not improbable that theirs was the double peninsula between Beauly and Bonar Bridge at the head of Dornoch Firth. Mr. Bradley, if I understand him aright, finds reasons for placing Ptolemy's Decantæ beyond Dornoch Firth. This means that the eastern aspect of the country from the Kyle of Sutherland to the extreme end of

Caithness was divided between no less than three tribes, the Decantæ, the Lugi, and the Smertæ; thus it follows that they must have been comparatively small tribes. One must, therefore, in the case of those on the corresponding extent of the west coast not be too ready to assume that the number assigned to the latter region by the manuscripts of Ptolemy's geography is greatly in excess of what the author actually wrote. Rather are we to infer that, for some reason unknown to us, his information concerning the northern extremity of the island was more minute than one could have been led to expect. Possibly this might be ascribed to the exploration carried out by Agricola's fleet. In any case the information here must have reached him through a Celtic channel, as is proved by such a name as Cornavii; nay, that Celtic channel can be more narrowly defined to have been Brythonic as distinguished from Goidelic, as can be shown from the name of the Decantæ. The interest attaching to this must be my excuse for going into a few details.

The name Decantæ occurs in the oldest manuscript of the Annales Cambriæ in the slightly different form of Decanti, as forming part of the place-name *Arx Decantorum*, or Hill-fort of the Decanti, now called Degannwy; its remains are to be seen on a hill near Llandudno and the mouth of the Conwy. The later Welsh name of Degannwy derives its form from an early Decantovion or Decantovia, according as the gender was neuter or feminine, but the origin of the word must be the same as that of the form Decanti. Now this name, whether the Decanti of the Llandudno peninsula were aborigines or invaders from Ireland, was a great name in that island, especially in Munster, as the Ogam inscriptions of that province go to prove. The Goidelic form they show is the genitive Decceti, as part of the designation of chiefs called, in the same case, *Maqui Decceti*, or Son of Dechet; for *cc* in the orthography of the old inscriptions was a digraph borrowed from the Brythons to express the sound of the spirant guttural *ch*. A tombstone of Maccu Decceti is still to be seen in Anglesey, and is so written in Roman capitals, whereas the same name occurs on a stone found in the vicinity of Tavistock in Devon, written Macco

Decheti, with the later Brythonic digraph *ch* used in spelling it. The situation of these two stones is a sufficient indication of the great activity of this tribe of invaders, whose ravages of Britain extended from Mona to the heart of Devon; but what interests us most directly at this point is the fact that their chiefs, from one generation to another, have the same designation of Macco Decheti, that is probably *the* Mac Dechet, just as Ireland still has men styled '*the* Mac Dermot,' '*the* O'Connor Don,' '*the* O'Donoghue,' and the like names distinguished by the use of the definite article. Now *Decheti* in early Irish and *Decanti* from a Brythonic source point back distinctly to a common source *Decenti*, which, according to the well-established habits of phonology prevalent in Irish and Welsh respectively, must yield *Dechet* and *Decant*, the latter of which is the form we have in Ptolemy's name of the Sutherland Decantæ. So much of the Celtic forms of these names and their pronunciation, but, when we come to the question of their origin, I am unable to say whether that was Celtic or not. In any case it is very remarkable that a people in the part which was the most certainly Pictish of this island should have been called Decantæ, that is to say Decheti, and that a powerful people of southern Ireland should have had as their chieftains men styled individually Macco Decheti. The inference I draw is that they were also of the same non-Aryan race, a fact which there is every reason already for assuming in the case of the Ivernians of Munster. The name Macco Decheti implies the individual name Dechet, and this, as a matter of fact, is known to Irish literature in the form of Techet as, for instance, in the name of a lake called Loch Techet. The Irish legends in which Techet figures offer nothing which would be contradictory of the supposition, that Techet was an ancestor—a god ancestor, most probably—of the aborigines.

We now come to the tribes on this side of the Caledonians, and the first in importance are the Vacomagi, who have no less than four towns assigned to them, namely, Banatia, supposed to have been at Buchanty on the river Almond, Tamea at a remarkable spot known as Inch Tuthill, near

Caputh, on the north side of the river Tay; thirdly, a place called the Winged Camp, which is supposed to have stood on the promontory of Burghead; and lastly, Tuessis, supposed to have been on the river Spey, near Boharm. Below the Vacomagi, and conterminous with them, were two peoples, the Vernicones, already mentioned, and to the north-east of the Vernicones the Tæxali. To these last he assigns one town called Devana, whose name and position indicate an inland site near the Dee: the remains of an ancient town near the Pass of Ballater, and close to Loch Daven, have been supposed to mark the spot. The Tæxali would seem to have inhabited the whole tract represented by the present county of Aberdeen; how much more, it is impossible to say. I should, however, be inclined to suppose that they extended to the Spey, and to give them a boundary in that direction coinciding roughly with that of Buchan and Marr on the side of Moray, and not wholly different from the western boundary of the present county of Banff. On the side of the Vernicones the question is still more difficult, as the history of Alban since Ptolemy's time does not lead us to expect the same comparative permanence of ancient landmarks in the basin of the Tay, or even in Angus and Mearns. So one might draw the boundary along the hills that continue the Mounth towards the sea between Stonehaven and Aberdeen, or treat one of the Esks as the division, or else, extend the domain of the Tæxali down to the Sidlaw Hills and the Firth of Tay. This last is perhaps the best hypothesis, and it coincides with Mr. Henry Bradley's conclusions, which make the Tæxali extend from the Tay Firth to the mouth of the Spey.

To take a more comprehensive survey of Ptolemy's tribes of North Britain, one cannot help being struck by the length of his list of them as compared with the summary allusions to them by Tacitus, Dio Cassius, and Ammianus Marcellinus. The tribes outside and beyond the Cisgrampian region are included by Dio under the simple designation of Caledonii, and by Ammianus under that of Dicalydonæ, are we then to suppose that they had sunk their differences and amalgamated into one people in the lapse of years between Ptolemy's time and that to which Dio Cassius refers? Hardly. One would come probably nearer the truth by supposing them more divided than Dio suggests, and more united than Ptolemy would lead one to infer at first sight. For not only does Dio speak of them under the single name of Caledonii, but the same manner of speaking is virtually postulated by Tacitus when he calls their common country Caledonia; the same is the inference from the term Dicalydonæ used by Ammianus, as it gives a collective force to a word referring to two sets of Caledonians, or the inhabitants of two Caledonian regions. Whatever the exact meaning of this Celtic, nay probably Brythonic, compound may have been, it seems to show that the Celts regarded the peoples beyond them as to a certain extent united among themselves. This is to be detected also in Ptolemy's adjective, Δουηκαληδόνιος, which he applies to the sea washing the shores of the Western Highlands. On the other hand it is not surprising that he should attempt to give us an exhaustive list of the tribes, since his business was geographical rather than political; but it is only accidentally that he allows his readers to discover that a part of his Albion was called ἡ Βρεττανία, namely that in which London was situated.

This in no way touches the difficulty attaching to the identity of the two sets of natives who gave rise to the Duecaledonian designation; for in the first place it is hard to understand the boundaries of Ptolemy's Caledonians. Their seaboard in the direction of Loch Fyne must be regarded as somewhat indefinite, for when he proceeds to speak of the Epidii as the next to the Dummonii towards the north-west, no allusion is made to the Caledonians coming in like a sort of wedge between them. In the next place the Caledonian Forest is said by him to have been above the Caledonians, but it is not quite certain how he looked at his map; on the whole, however, he seems to have regarded the forest as forming a part or the whole of the boundary between the Caledonians and the tribes beyond them on the west coast. In the attempt to trace the western boundary of the Caledonians as between them and the coast tribes, one is lost in the mountain region between Ben Nevis and the upper course of the Farrar, at the mouth of which, under the name of Beauly, we are enabled to detect the Caledonians a second time, thanks to the geographer's express statement that they extended to the mouth of the Varar. The boundary between them and the Vacomagi is still more hopeless, and if the Caledonians were conterminous with the Dumnonians in the south-west of the former's territory, they probably reached the fringe of the forest extending across the country from Menteith to Dunkeld ; but as one proceeds from Loch Lomond in a north-easterly direction one comes upon the Vacomagi on the Almond, so that if they were posted there, one would not unnaturally expect to find them in possession of the greater part or the whole of Athole westwards to Loch Lomond.

Now, Ptolemy gives the Caledonians neither an intelligible frontier towards the Vacomagi nor the possession of a single town or stronghold, and altogether one looks in vain in his pages for any indication of the Caledonians as such being at any time of sufficient importance to have given their name to Caledonia. On the other hand the Vacomagi held the southern border of the forest dividing the Brythons of Fortrenn from them and kept up a challenge to the latter on the banks of the Almond, while they had a position on the Tay at a point below Dunkeld. Judging from the number of towns assigned them by Ptolemy—and they were the only Transgrampian people who had any towns at all except the Tæxali, who had one—it looks as if they could have had no rivals in the Highlands at the time to which Ptolemy's account applies. It is natural therefore to regard them as the people to give its collective name to the northern Pictland and not his Caledonians. The explanation therefore is that either the Caledonians had once been more powerful than the Vacomagi and better known to the Celts ; or else—and this is the more probable theory—both Ptolemy's Caledonii and Vacomagi were equally entitled to the name of Caledonians. The Caledonians of Ptolemy were, I take it, divided into two tribes or branches, of which the one was called Vacomagi while no distinctive name for the other has reached us; it was unknown also probably to Ptolemy. In other words Ptolemy's Caledonii and Vacomagi were both Caledonians, and they were the peoples implied by the terms Duecaledonius and Dicalydonæ, which refer to two sets of Caledonians or the inhabitants of two Caledonians. That the Vacomagi were as much Caledonians as the others is rendered highly probable by the fact, among other things, of the still existing name of a strong position, which must have been one of the most important in their possession : I allude to that of Dunkeld, which literally means the dún or fortress of the Caledonians, though it was in the country of the Vacomagi. Further, if you will look at Dr. Skene's map of 'Scotland with the ancient Divisions of the Land' in the third volume of his *Celtic Scotland*, you will find that the territory of Ptolemy's Caledonii, plus that of his Vacomagi, which one may collectively speak of as Duecaledonian, coincides, roughly speaking, with his Moray and Ross, together with Athole. At any rate that will do if you allow a certain margin for the forest separating Athole from Fortrenn, and also for contingencies, in the direction of the Decantæ, arising out of the difficulty, already indicated as attaching to the question of their exact locality, and of the impossibility of ascertaining the date of their subjugation by the Duecaledonian power. Further, all the southern lands owned by the Picts fell away from them when their power was broken in the region of the Tay, and then Athole appears with an individuality of its own. How much of Gowrie should be regarded as having had a similar history is not clear. But after the well known and crushing defeat inflicted by Angus king of Fortrenn, on Nechtan and his Picts, on the banks of the Spey, in the year 729, the Northerners never obtained a firm footing south of the Grampians until Macbeth succeeded in establishing himself there for a time.

Everything points to the fact that the strength of his race lay in the country bearing the dual appellation of Moray and Ross. These were divided from one another by the river Beauly, and it is possible—I will not say probable—that the duality of Moray and Ross was but a continuation of the duality echoed by such early forms as Duecaledonius and Dicalydonæ. The application of the former by Ptolemy to the sea on the west of Scotland is very remarkable, as it argues the paramount importance sometime or other of a people or group of peoples of Duecaledonii, whose existence as such is completely ignored in his pages. It is possible that the tribes on the west coast owned allegiance even then to those occupying the country afterwards known as Moray and Ross, and that the latter ruled down to the sea. The earliest information on this point is, that the Dalriad Scots, having taken possession of a large extent of the west coast, were driven back into Cantyre by Brude mac Maelchon, the Pictish king, to whom St. Columba paid a visit at his headquarters somewhere near Inverness. The Dalriad Scots were Christians, under the powerful protection of their kinsman Columba, and the object of his mission to the Pictish king was probably to intercede for his people, as well as to convert the heathen Picts to the Christian faith. In this latter object he and his coadjutors are said to have been successful, but it does not appear that the saint obtained any immediate advantages for the Dalriad Scots, as we read of the latter sustaining another defeat, attended by the death of their king, at the hands of the Picts at a battle fought in Cantyre in 574. However, Brude seems to have either given St. Columba the Isle of Iona, or to have confirmed him in the possession of it. Now, Cantyre and Iona are both far from Inverness, and the allusion to them here will serve to elucidate what Bæda has left on record, when he terms Brude a most powerful king.

His dominions extended in other directions likewise. The Decantæ and the other small tribes occupying the country beyond Ross were probably all subject to him, as it is known that the Orkneys were. This rests on the testimony of Adamnan, who says that Columba met the regulus of Orkney at Brude's court, and asked Brude to bid him receive favourably some of the Saint's fellow-missionaries who had set out on a dangerous voyage to Orkney. This he was in a position to do, we are told, as the regulus was subject to Brude, who had his hostages then in his hands. Thus it would seem that all Alban beyond the Grampians owned the sway of the Picts of Moray and Ross from Cantyre round to the Orkneys: the only region whose history is a matter of mere guess is that from the Spey to the Firth of Tay, but it is not impossible that this also was more or less subject to the same Pictish power. Then as to the banks of the Tay, it is known that the advancing arms of the Brythons of Fortrenn were not able finally to dislodge the Picts there till the contest between Angus and Nechtan in the 8th century. Arguing backwards therefore to the time of Ptolemy, the Duecaledonii must have been one of the two most powerful nations beyond the Forth, and they without doubt exercised far the widest sway there; so that there is nothing to surprise one in the fact, that it is they who gave its name to the country and to the sea beyond.

Before closing these remarks let us for a moment examine the principal names concerned, those of the Vacomagi and the Duecaledonii. The former of these appears to be a compound Brythonic adjective connoting empty plains or empty fields; it would thus seem at first sight as though the Caledonians termed Vacomagi by their Celtic neighbours, had that name given them in reference to the poverty of the soil of a great part of their country; but it is a somewhat serious objection to this interpretation to find that the territory of the Vacomagi included most of the best land in the north, such, for example, as that of the district between the Ness and the Spey. Let us therefore try another tack; the empty plains or fields implied by the name of the Vacomagi may have referred to them simply as empty in the sense of being free from forest. According to this interpretation, which is quite legitimate and natural, the name might be explained practically to have meant much the same thing as if they were termed Strath Men or inhabitants of the level country; but it lays on us the burden of answering some such a question as how a name of this kind could have been applied to a people occupying the southern fringe of the forest from Loch Lomond to Dunkeld, together with the Highland region immediately behind that line. The only answer to such a question is that the people called Vacomagi must have received that name while they were as yet dwellers of the more level country: in other words they are to be regarded as the representatives of native lowlanders, who had been robbed of their country and driven for refuge to the forests and the mountains by the advance of the Aryan as represented by the Mæatæ, the Men of Fortrenn of a period which for Britain must be treated as pre-historic. Let us now turn to the other term in question, to wit, the name Dicalidonæ used by Ammianus: this, as it has already been hinted, refers us in a sort of way, to two groups of Caledonians; but a far more ancient, and—I would add—a far more correct form is to be extracted from Ptolemy's Δουηκαληδόνιος 'Ωκεανός, backed as it is by the later geographer Marcian. In the adjective one recognizes the antecedent of the Welsh feminine *dwy*, corresponding to the masculine *dau* 'two,' and one obtains from Ptolemy's adjective a Due-Caledon, which would be in modern Welsh Dwy Gelyddon or the 'Two Caledonias.' The gender is important to notice, as it shows that the Brythons spoke not of two kinds of Caledonians but of two Caledonias with their inhabitants, in both instances, Caledonians alike. It is needless to remind you that this is not the first instance we have found of the names of the remoter peoples of Britain reaching the authors of antiquity through the medium of the Brythonic inhabitants of the south-eastern portion of the island. So far so well; but what, according to Brythonic ideas, did the two Caledonias consist of?

To have reached the Brython it must have been some broad distinction, some distinction which would be widely patent to the south; and this, I think, is indicated by the name of the Vacomagi connecting them in an earlier stage of their history with the plains of the Lowlands. That was the one Caledonia, the more level and clear Caledonia of straths and carses: the other was the Caledonia stern and wild of the Highlands of the north and west. The original owners of the former country had retreated into the Highland Caledonia, but they were as truly Caledonian as those whom Ptolemy called Caledonians, though they had come to be known by a name distinguishing them as those who had come from the Lowland Caledonia of clear plains.

All this implies a state of things differing considerably from the picture I drew of them when I began to study early Scotland: then I regarded the positions held by the Vacomagi on the Tay and the Almond as the advanced posts of a conquest tending southward from the direction of Inverness and the Moray Firth, whereas now I should be more inclined to regard them as the last posts held by the rear of a force conducting a retreat northward; so that when Angus and the Men of Fortrenn defeated Nechtan and took possession of the Pictish positions on the Tay, and when somewhat later they caused the death of the king of Athole, all this is to be regarded as the later terms in the series of Celtic encroachments, in the course of which the Mæatæ had forced the Vacomagi into the forests near the Highland Line. This hypothesis, for it is but a hypothesis, seems on the whole to be free from several objections to which the other was open, and to be in harmony with the tenor of the later fortunes of Alban.

A history which is so precarious and scrappy as that of ancient Britain, is considerably helped by any identification of an old name with its modern representative, in such a way as to give the former some fixity of place. The case of the name of the Verturiones has been duly signalized; but I have one or two more to mention which have suggested themselves to me since the earlier portion of this lecture was put together. They seem too important to be compressed into a note, so I venture to discuss them at this point. Last September I had the pleasure of spending some time at Kennet, on the other side of the Forth, when Lord Balfour of Burleigh took me to see various places of interest in the neighbourhood of the Ochil Hills. As my mind was full of the question how and where the ancient Brythons had settled beyond the Forth, I was, though I am ashamed to confess it, less charmed with the beauty of the scenery I saw than exercised by the sound of the place-names I heard. As the first in order but not in importance may be mentioned the name Ochil itself. The loftiest of the Ochil Hills is said to be Bencleuch, with a height of 2363 feet, which is not a remarkable elevation for Scotland; but as the Ochils rise almost from the level of the sea, and as they appear to advantage in point of mass and height when looked at from the south, they may well have been known to the Brythons on this side of the Forth as the High Hills; so the prevalent etymology identifying *Ochil* with the Welsh word *uchel* 'high,' may be treated as correct, until a more convincing one is proposed. The westernmost peak over against Stirling sinks to about half the height of Bencleuch; but it affords one of the best views in the kingdom, and it is known by a name which I should phonetically describe as Dŭmyat or D'myat, with its *my* strongly accented but otherwise pronounced like the pronoun *my*. The sound of the word roused my curiosity, as it indicated a Celtic name made up of two words in syntactic relation to one another, and I learned from Lord Balfour, who owns the hill, that the spelling he has found in his estate papers is *Dunmyat:* since then I have noticed that in the New Statistical Account it is printed Demyat and even Damiett, and that in Black's *Guide to Scotland* it is given as *Dun-myat.* Whilst I have been occupied with these points connected with the modern form, you will have anticipated me in the interpretation to be put upon it: beyond all doubt it must mean the *dún* or fort of Myat, that is to say of the Miati or Mæatæ. Whether there are any traces of the *dún* still to be seen, and where exactly they are situated on the hill, is a question which I must leave to Scotch archæology. Here at any rate we have one locality with which we can venture to associate the ancient Mæatæ: or more accurately speaking it is one in addition to that denoted by the name of Fortrenn, from which they may be treated as inseparable under their other name of Verturiones.

But whether we call them Mæatæ or Verturiones, they were merely an outlying portion of the larger tribe of the Dumnonii: they were in fact the aggressive Dumnonii who undertook to extend the dominion of their people northwards. So there would be nothing surprising in their being known also simply as Dumnonii. Now this was likewise the name of a people in the south-west of Britain, and there we know what has become of it, namely, that it has yielded the county of Devon its English name, in modern Welsh *Dyvnaint*. So we know approximately what sort of name to expect in the north, where it can scarcely be an accident that we have, in the Perthshire portion of the Ochils, a parish called Glen*devon*, whence the river Devon takes its circuitous course to the Firth of Forth near Alloa. In Glendevon is also the pass through which Montrose marched in 1645, when he came down like a wolf on Castle Campbell. It would be interesting to know whether the site of that castle was fortified in early times, as it can only have been held by men who were masters of the Ochils above it. Now if one put together the fact of the position of Dunmyat and Fortrenn, and of the towns of the northern Dumnonii as placed by Ptolemy; also the negative fact that he assigns them no position on the northern banks of the Forth, one discovers a sure clue to the line of their northward advance. When they had become masters of the country between Dumbarton and Stirling, they pushed on sooner or later along the valleys and straths now followed by the railway from Stirling and the Bridge of Allan to Forteviot and Perth; thereby they avoided the necessity of crossing any high mountains. When they had acquired possession of that line of country, they had practically got round the Picts dwelling between the Ochils and the Forth, and their position on Dunmyat must have been meant to overawe them. At a more eastern point they appear to have ultimately crossed the Ochils, and threatened the Picts on the lower banks of the Devon; in fact it looks as if the entire range of the Ochils had come into their hands, placing the Picts between it and the Forth wholly at their mercy, though that river would seem to have effectually served the Picts as their southern barrier. To return to the identification suggested of Glendevon with the Dumnonii, it is right to say, that it requires the river Devon to have been so called from the upland district in the Ochils, and the Black Devon after the Devon; so we are here on ground, which is less safe, than that on which the connection of Dunmyat with the Mæatæ so firmly rests.

THE SPREAD OF GAELIC IN SCOTLAND.

IN this lecture I propose to deal with the extremely difficult question of the origin and history of Goidelic speech in the north of this island. Are we to regard it wholly and entirely as a language introduced from Ireland, or are we to treat it as of older standing in the North? In order to answer this, let us recall the view put forward as to the origin of Goidelic speech such as it is found in Ireland itself. It was described as an Aryan language of the Q group influenced to a considerable extent by an Aryan language of the P group, and influenced also by contact with a non-Aryan tongue. It was further conjectured that the conquest of Erinn by the Celts began with that of ancient Meath; and so far as concerns the account briefly suggested of the genesis of Irish Goidelic, it is enough to postulate the conditions implied once for all in Meath and on the opposite coast of Britain, somewhere between the Solway Firth and the Severn Sea. It would be hazardous to postulate the same conditions along the whole frontier land of Brythonic conquest. For example, it does not follow that wherever the Brythons made conquests in Britain, exactly the same regions must have been previously in the possession of Goidels: suppose, for example, as we have already done, that the Brythons extended their invasion to the valley of the Tay, we should be under no necessity to assume the Goidels to have preceded them there; nor can I find any reason in fact to believe that the Brythons at first had intercourse in Fortrenn or anywhere north of the Forth with any other people than the native Picts. If, as is probable, an amalgamation between the ruling Brythons and the subject Picts of Fortrenn took place, the result would be a language consisting of Brythonic influenced by Pictish or else Pictish influenced by Brythonic: which of the two it would prove to be, would depend on the relative forces of civilization as well as on the force of arms of the races concerned. As a matter of fact we are not left altogether in the dark as to what did happen there in this respect: the resultant speech was Brythonic, but if we 'may judge of it by the few specimens left, it differed, as in Bæda's *Pean-fahel*, more from the other Brythonic dialects than they differ from one another: that difference is therefore probably to be in great part ascribed to Pictish influence; but with the fall of the Fortrenn dynasty, and the rise of that of Kenneth MacAlpin and his Goidelic supporters, that kind of Brythonic speech perished, leaving us now without an adequate idea, what a Brythonic language in Pictish mouths would be exactly like.

Let us take another point of view: the Brythons, coming from the Continent later than the Goidels, stood nearer to Continental culture whatever it was, so that they may be presumed to have been better armed, and therefore able to push their conquest of Britain further, as against the aboriginal inhabitants, than their forerunners of the Goidelic branch had succeeded in doing. So far then we seem to have no warrant for supposing Goidelic to have been of ancient standing in the North; and as for any direct proof of its existence there in the time of Agricola or of Ptolemy, there is absolutely none that I know. We have, therefore, to show, if possible, how and when Goidelic speech was brought into Scotland. This is in part comparatively easy, as the immigration of the Dalriad Scots was an event of history. Now the territory of the Dalriad Scots in Britain was called not only Airer Dalriatai ('the Border belonging to the Dalriads'), and Oirer Alban ('the Border of Britain'), but also Airer Gaethel, a name of which there were various abbreviated forms, one of which has yielded the modern *Argyle*: it means the Goidels' Border, that is to say, the border or fringe belonging to the Goidels: it has been rendered into Latin by Margo Scottorum, or the March of the Goidels, meaning in this instance the Goidelic settlers from Dalriada in the north-east of Ireland; and it implies not only the introduction of Goidelic speech from the sister island, but also that the region beyond the border occupied by the immigrants was inhabited by a people who were not Goidels, a people characterized by the use of a language other than Goidelic: this was doubtless the Pictish of the aboriginal inhabitants.

The settlement of the Dalriad Scots in Argyle brought them in time into collision with the ruling Picts; and it is supposed, as already hinted in another lecture, that the trouble arising in consequence was one of the reasons why St. Columba visited the Pictish king Brude, in the neighbourhood of Inverness. He is said to have baptized Brude and converted his people to the Christian faith. To say the least of it, he laid the way open for the missionaries of his church to extend their labours to the northern Picts, to whom they became teachers. Among the things which the Columban clergy taught the Picts was doubtless their own Goidelic language. As to the extent to which the Dalriad settlers propagated the same in the west, the data are very precarious; but we read that they spread themselves far beyond Cantyre, and that Brude had to drive them back into Cantyre However, it is not improbable that they took possession later of most of the west coast as far as Loch Broom or thereabouts. This may have been merely an expansion of their influence rather than anything like a conquest by force of arms. At any rate the later history of Alban teaches us that Airer Gaethel or Argyle was divided into, or considered to consist of, two parts, namely, the Argyle, belonging to Scotia or the kingdom of Scone, and this would be the more southern portion of Argyle, corresponding more or less to the present county of that name; the other was the Argyle belonging to Moravia or Moray: this would be the northern strip reaching to the vicinity of Loch Broom. Here we have indications how all the western coast became Goidelic, and how the influence of Goidelic speech may have spread into Moray and the heart of the Pictish country of the North. Strange to say, the Norsemen probably helped the later spread of Goidelic from Man to Shetland, for though they seem to have always retained their own Norse, the chief language of their thralls on the west coast appears to have been Goidelic, so that as soon as the Norse master disappears, Goidelic has the ground to itself. This is perhaps to be accounted for in part by the fact that their thralls consisted, possibly to no inconsiderable extent, of men carried away from Ireland.

Let us now return to Columba at Brude's Court near the Ness, where the capital of the Highlands may be said to have been, even as it is still. We hear nothing of any difficulty of speech between the saint and the king or his noblés; but we do hear a little later of Columba preaching by interpreter to a peasant and his family somewhere, as it would seem, in the neighbourhood of the Pictish king's headquarters. Similarly, when Columba happened to be staying in the island of Skye, two young men come by sea bringing their father in a dying state to the saint, who preaches to the dying man by interpreter, and baptizes him. He was a pagan and the chief, as he is called, of the *Geona Cohors*, which I have associated in another lecture with Cruithne's eponymous son Ce. St. Columba's convert was probably a Pict of the same race as Brude himself, and the representative of the power of that race on the mainland over against Skye. Neither there nor in the neighbourhood of Inverness is there any reason to suppose any Celtic tongue prevalent at that time, except in so far as the Scots had introduced their Goidelic, which was the saint's own language.

The Dalriad Scots had come over to Britain towards the end of the fifth century under Fergus Mór mac Erca, but the chief organiser of their state was his great-grandson, Aidan son of Gabran, who was helped to the kingship in no small degree by Columba, who saw in him the making of a strenuous leader. Let us take the scanty references to Aidan in the Irish Chronicles. in order. In 574, he is made king of the Dalriad Scots; in 579 and 580, we read of engagements of Aidan's in Orkney, whither he would seem to have undertaken an expedition. In 581, Baedan mac Cairill died, who was king of the Ulidians or Irish Picts, and wielded so much power that he is referred to in Irish literature as deriving tribute from Munster, Connaught, Skye, and Man; he is also represented as receiving the hostages of Aidan at Ros na Rig in Semne, which is now called Island Magee, near Larne in Antrim. He also had troops over in this country engaged in opposing the Angles in Manann, a

district which we cannot better define than by a vague
reference to the positions of Sla*mannan* or the Hills of
Manann, and Clack*mannan*, so called from the sacred Stone
of Manann, now more commonly associated with the Bruce.
Perhaps we are to understand chiefly by the Plain of Manann
the land skirting the Forth, especially between Stirling
and the Pentland Hills; but whatever it exactly comprised,
Baedan is said to have cleared it of the Angles, and to have retained possession of it until his death. Brythons, Dalriad Scots,
and Ulidian Picts, at various times combined to oppose the advance of the Angles, and to contest the possession of one of the
finest sites for a city in the whole world, that of this great historic
Edinburgh of yours. The combination appears to have been
joined by Aidan during the lifetime of Baedan mac Cairill.
Aidan had here probably some claim based, as one may suppose,
on the fact of a settlement of Dalriad Scots somewhere in these
parts, as there probably was also of Ulidian Cruithni or Picts
from Ireland. In 582, one reads of Aidan fighting a battle in
Manann, in which he was victorious, but hardly anything
else is known. In 590, one reads also of a battle of Leithrig,
in which he was engaged, but with what result or even
against what foe, one is not told. Then we come to the battle of
Circinn in 596, in which Aidan is said to have prevailed, but at
the expense of losing four of his sons: this was the war of the
Miati, as Adamnan calls it. Soon after this, Aidan's patron and
friend, Columba, died; and we pause next with the year 603,
under which a great war with the Angles is mentioned, in which
Aidan, assisted by Maeluma, son of Baedan mac Cairill, at the
head of the Ulidian Picts, was defeated in a great battle by
Æthelfrith and his Angles: according to Bæda, it was fought at
a place called Degsastan. Lastly, Aidan died in the year 606,
when he was 74 years of age, and when he had been king for 38
years. I have incidentally mentioned Baedan, who was not king
of Ulster in the wider sense, but of the Ulidians, the True
Ultonians or the non-Celtic peoples of the North of Ireland. Now
the story of the power he enjoyed is hardly intelligible except
on the supposition, that he was the head of some sort of federa-

tion of a group of the ancient inhabitants, who happened to be still more or less independent.

Such is a brief account of Aidan, and such are the glimpses it gives of the great activity, in his days, of the Dalriad Scots, and to a less degree of their neighbours and kinsmen the Ulidian Picts or Cruithni. Not only had both of them settlements in the neighbourhood probably of the Firth of Forth, but the Dalriad Scots, so far from contenting themselves with their other territories, made expeditions by sea as far as the Orkneys. Their object in these expeditions is not very clear, but they were probably in search of new settlements, or defending settlements already made by their kinsmen. This renders it not incredible that the war of the Miati, in which Aidan fought the battle of Circinn, took place, if not in the district called Circinn, and comprising Angus and the Mearns, at any rate somewhere in the Cisgrampian district beyond the Forth. The site of that battle is very important, as it affords a sort of indication where to look for a settlement of the Scots beyond the Forth. That settlement should prove, wherever it was, a focus from which Goidelic speech was propagated among the Picts east and south of the Grampians; for the Dalriad Scots brought with them as their language, the Goidelic which became the Gaelic of Scotland in the modern sense of the word.

Here, as elsewhere not unfrequently in the history of this country, we have to reason backwards from ascertained facts to a state of things anterior to them, and less adequately recorded, if at all. We set out from the history of the Kenneth mac Alpin dynasty and their central dominion on the Tay: from them and that district Gaelic was propagated during the whole period of their rule. Before the triumph of Kenneth, the unsuccessful supporters of the claim of his race to rule belonged to the same region so far back as we can trace them. This brings us to the time of Aidan, who seemingly found Scots already settled there, or else founded a settlement of Scots there by direct interference, involving presumably his fighting the battle of Circinn. This is countenanced by the fact that the Scottic dynasty of Kenneth traced its pedigree back to Aidan. Thus the Tripartite life of St. Patrick makes the saint address Fergus Mór in the following words :—" Though thy brother has not much regard for thee to-day, it is thou who shalt be king: from thee shall be the kings in this land and in Fortrenn for ever,' to which is added the remark, 'and this was fulfilled in Aidan, son of Gabran, who took Alban by force.' Similarly, a tract on the Picts, written, according to Dr. Skene, before the year 1373, refers to the Scots as belonging to the tribes of Thrace, which probably meant the story connecting *Scotti* with *Scythia*, and speaks of their clearing for themselves a sword-land among the Brythons. This is explained to mean the Plain of Fortrenn first and the Plain of Circinn afterwards. Here the mention of the Swordland in the Plain of Circinn refers to the quartering by the Kenneth dynasty of some of its representatives in the Mearns, and from a passage in the Pictish Chronicle it is known that Fetteresso or Fodresach, in the parish of Fordun in the Mearns, was in the Swordland here in question. Putting this aside, the earlier Swordland of the Scots was among the Brythons and in Fortrenn : in other words, it was acquired at the expense of the Brythons of Fortrenn, who must accordingly be supposed to have also ruled or claimed to rule over the central region of the Tay, that is, roughly speaking, the province of Gowrie. Here was Scone, which became the capital of the Scots, and at Scone was preserved the Lia Fáil, the so-called Stone of Destiny : it was the palladium of the Scot, and believed to have been brought from Tara in Ireland. Whether this was the real history of the celebrated stone at Scone, now supposed to be in the Coronation Chair at Westminster, or not, it is highly probable that the Scots, when they settled at Scone, did bring their palladium with them. The question of the credibility of the legend in its entirety is a matter of minor importance, but great interest attaches to it as an indication, whence the makers of the kingdom of Scone were supposed to have come.

The recorded settlement of the Dalriad Scots in force in Argyle in the fifth century was probably by no means their first coming over to the north of Britain, and we may have to place the beginning of the immigrations of the Ulidian Picts somewhat earlier still; altogether this is a matter of much greater uncertainty than the movements of the Scots. It is, however, to them that we are perhaps to refer the name of the river Earn and that of Loch Earn and Strath Earn. On this point I may mention a saint Foelan or Faolan, who is called in hagiological documents Foelan of Ráth Erann, that is, of the Fort of the Erna or the Ivernians. Now, St. Foelan is supposed to have left his name to the parish of St. Fillans, at the east end of Loch Earn, and the church of Aberdour in Fife is dedicated to him. He flourished about the beginning of the sixth century; and besides his churches in North Britain he had one in Leinster, and he is described as of the race of Aengus Nadfraech, king of Munster. Now, did the saint's establishment prove of sufficient importance to give his name not only to St. Fillans but also to account for a new name being given to the loch, the river, and the strath? In case it did, it would go some way to account for the introduction of Goidelic speech into that neighbourhood, as Goidelic is likely to have been at the time, if not the prevailing language of Foelan's people, at least their fashionable language. The more probable account, however, is that Foelan chose the district of the Earn for the scene of his labours as already containing a population of Ivernians from Ireland. It was a long way from Munster to Athole, but so it was from Emly, for instance, with which the name of Foelan's teacher, Ailbe, is associated, and Emly, though somewhat more south than Tipperary without being far west of it, happens to be specially mentioned as a place which owned the sway of Baedan mac Cairill. However, we are by no means obliged to suppose that the Erna from whom Ráth Erann took its name, must have come from the spot where that name is attested, as it is possible that it was borne also by kindred tribes in the northern half of Ireland. Lastly, another pupil of Ailbe was Colman of Druim-Mór, who settled in one of the islets in the Lake of Menteith, called Inis Mocholmóg, now Inchmahome.

In this connection may be also mentioned, that Irish pedigrees trace back to the seed of an Eber, son of Ir, a family which they call the Eoganacht of Mag Gerginn in Alban; that is to say, those descendants of a great ancestor Eogan, who had found their home in the Mearns. There were in Ireland itself several tribes of Eoganachts or descendants of a mythic Eogan, as for instance, those who gave their name to Tir Eogan, 'the land of Eogan,' now made into Tyrone, as the English name of a county in the north of Ireland. Irish pedigrees also trace Macbeth back to ancestors in Ireland, while they speak, in quite another direction, of a *Clann Conaill Cirr mic Echach Buidhe* as the Men of Fife, which means that a certain ruling family or families in Fife were derived from a well-known ancestor in Ireland. All this goes to show that adventurers from Ireland found their way into the heart of the Pictish country and sometimes settled there. They possibly brought with them not only an intrepid spirit but also a skill in war superior to that which had as yet been acquired by the Picts of the North. But be that as it may, the fact of the intercourse between Ireland and Britain is not to be doubted: it is to be seen on almost every page of Irish literature, and it probably means intercourse mainly with the Picts of Alban both on the west coast and inland as far as the watershed and across to the Moray Firth, not with the Brythons of Fortrenn, the conquerors of some of the Picts and the natural enemies of the whole race. The primary cause of the emigration from Ireland may be supposed to have been the Celtic conquests in that country, especially after the native Ivernians, known as Ulidians or True Ultonians, had been driven out of Oriel and crowded into the north-east corner, between Loch Neagh and the sea. This would take us back beyond the middle of the fourth century, if we may rely on the year 333 as that of the conquests of Oriel by the Three Collas, and from that time the emigration of adventurers to Britain might probably be expected. That we cannot be far wrong in this surmise is proved by the fact that the Scotti appear by name in the history of Roman Britain for the first time not long afterwards, to wit, in the year 360: thus we learn from the pages of Ammianus that the Scotti joined in the determined attack then made on the Roman Province by the Picts, a name under which we are, as early as the year 306, made familiar with the Caledonians and other peoples of the North. Once this career of plundering the Roman dominions had been entered upon by the natives of the north or the north-east of Ireland, there would be no limit to the area over which the movement might be recruited; all the North of Ireland would probably come under the influence of its attraction, all the West as far south as the Shannon, and possibly a good deal further.

The Picts welcomed their kinsmen from Ireland in their attacks on the Province; but was this likely to be the only kind of encouragement given them by the Picts? Hardly. The Picts had a long-standing feud with the Brythons of Fortrenn, whose encroachments must have always been a trouble to them. The Picts still held possession of certain strong positions on the Tay and the Almond. Accordingly Saint Columba, who had visited Brude at his northern headquarters, near the Moray Firth, can be traced not long after on the Tay with Brude's successor, Gartnait. The latter's headquarters are supposed to have been at Abernethy, where he was the restorer or, in some other way, the benefactor of a church dedicated there to St. Bridget of Kildare. The Saint is said to have taught the tribes on the Tay, and to have, with the support of the king, subdued all opposition there, whatever that may have exactly meant. Now, we find that Columba, who is not mentioned residing as teacher at the court of King Brude, seems to have been able at Gartnait's to pursue his work systematically: it is probable that on the Tay he found a population even then, with whom he could treat in his own Goidelic tongue. What the Picts of the North seem to have done with the immigrants from Ireland was this: they settled them on their southern boundary and on the Tay, where they were always in danger from the Brythons.

Thus they may have planted them at an early date, comparatively speaking, on the southern side of Athole and the border-lands of Fortrenn, including the district near and around Loch Earn. Still more important must be regarded the settling of them in Gowrie and the neighbourhood of the Firth of Tay, which drove as it were a Goidelic wedge right through the centre of the Cisgrampian country. The land thus granted to their Goidelic allies by the Picts was probably the border or marches immediately threatened by the Men of Fortrenn, who naturally lost no opportunity of seizing upon it, and the Miatic war, in which Aidan fought the battle of Circinn, can hardly have been unconnected with the contest going on between the Brythons, whose old name was that of Mæatæ or Miati, and the Picts or Caledonians on the Tay. Aidan was then introducing Goidels there for the first time, or else he was coming to the aid of Goidels already settled there. Granting either alternative to be in the main correct, one can understand how the Goidelic language spread over Athole, and how from Gowrie it gained ground in the course of time on both sides of the Tay. My theory briefly stated comes to this: the Picts allowed—perhaps invited—their Goidelic allies to settle on their marches to help them against their hereditary foes of Fortrenn. The Goidels or Scots did so, but in due time they contested—and successfully contested—the rule of their Pictish masters. This exactly fits in with the traditional account of Kenneth MacAlpin's victory: the Scots, according to that, acquired their power by massacring the nobles of the Picts, which closely resembles the Welsh story of the triumph of Hengist and his Jutes; and the similarity of the two legends seems to argue a similarity in the facts underlying them. But to bring evidence such as would directly establish the correctness of this view, is rendered impossible by the slenderness of our data. It only remains, therefore, to examine it in the light of the later history so as to see how far it explains the facts of that history.

Now, if the Scots were placed by the northern Picts on their frontiers to act against the Brythons, it is but natural to expect that, as they became firmly established on the Tay, far away from the Pictish base of operations, they would tend to assert their independence of the Picts and to fight for themselves. Supposing this to have become history, one might find at one time no less than four competitors for power in the Cisgrampian area. Thus there would be the Brythons, called successively Mæatæ, Verturiones and Men of Fortrenn; there would be the settlers on the Tay speaking Goidelic and called in Latin Scotti, whence their English designation of Scots; there would be the Picts of Circinn or Angus and the Mearns, representing the portion of the ancient Tæxali who dwelt this side of the Mounth, in the enjoyment possibly of the assistance of their kinsmen beyond it; and lastly, there would be the Northern Picts, who had access to the arena by way of Dunkeld and a retreat northwards open to them when worsted. We leave Gartnait, presumably of that race, in this district of the Tay, at the end of the sixth century: we have then to skip a whole century and more before the curtain lifts again to shew us a Northern Pict still wielding power in the Cisgrampian region. He bore the name of Nechtan, called Naitan by Bæda, who records his conforming in the year 710, to the Church of Rome, in the matter of observing Easter. The Columban clergy, refusing, however, to accept the change, were at length forced by Nechtan in 717 to leave his dominions, whereupon they crossed the mountains to their kinsmen the Dalriad Scots. This had doubtless the effect of alienating the whole Columban Church, and for some reason or other, Nechtan left his throne in 724 and became a cleric. The next king was a certain Drust, whose supporters were not at peace with Nechtan's friends, since we read of the latter capturing and binding Drust's son, Simal, in 725, which led Drust to retaliate on Nechtan. In the ensuing year a third competitor for power appears in the person of Alpin, son of Eochaid, and brother to another Eochaid. The brothers Alpin and Eochaid were Dalriad Scots, and they burst into activity simultaneously in 726, when Eochaid becomes king of Dalriada and Alpin proceeds to oust Drust from power in the region of the Tay, which he succeeds in doing, so that he becomes king there himself, that is, doubtless in the narrowest sense, king of the Scots on the Tay. A fourth competitor was watching his opportunity, namely, Ungust or Angus, king of the Men of Fortrenn, and in 728 a battle is fought between him and Alpin at Moncrieff, near the junction of the Earn and the Tay. In this battle Alpin was defeated and lost his son, while Angus' power was increased. Soon afterwards Alpin sustained a still more crushing defeat at the hands of Nechtan, who had returned to secular life. Alpin fled, leaving his men and his territory in the possession of Nechtan as the result of this battle, fought as it is supposed, at Scone. It is to be noticed that the sympathy of the Irish chronicler is recorded very decidedly in favour of Alpin, and doubtless the latter's men were the Goidels of Gowrie and Athole: both his battles were fought in the central region of the Tay, where he would seem to have commanded his chief support.

The next conflict is between Angus and Nechtan; the latter was, it would appear, retreating, for the battle between them was fought in 729, near a lake Lochdiæ, supposed to be Loch Inch formed by the waters of the river Spey, and Nechtan was completely routed, losing several of his chief men. Angus was now called king of the Picts, but it still remained for him to defeat Drust, which he did at a place called Druimderg Blathmig, identified with the headland called the Red Head of Angus. This would seem to indicate that the principal seat of Drust's power was Circinn, or the region of Angus and Mearns, that is, roughly speaking, the modern counties of Forfar and Kincardine.

After Alpin's failure, an attempt was made by another Scot, named Talorgan son of Congus, but he was defeated and driven over the mountains to seek refuge among the Dalriad Scots, like Alpin before him. As to Alpin, he died leader of the same Scots in 741, after their political existence had been put an end to by Angus, who saw in them a serious danger to his rule over Alban. Angus would seem to have also been resolved to keep a firm hand on Athole: at any rate we read under the year 729 of his having Talorgan, son of Drostan, king of Athole, put to death. But in another direction we find him founding the bishopric of St. Andrews, as if desirous of conciliating the people of Fife. Be that as it may, Angus secured for the Men of Fortrenn a power which they retained without much interruption till the middle of the ninth century; but a few more details as to the events of that long interval will be useful as completing the evidence of the close connection between the Dalriad Scots and the Scots on the Tay. In 768 an attempt was made to resuscitate the power of the Dalriad Scots by a certain Aed Finn. The latter waged war against Ciniod, son of Wredech, who was then king of the Picts; but Aed was defeated, and his death figures under the year 778. The next thing to notice is the occupation of the throne by Conall, son of Taidg, whose name Conall is decidedly Goidelic. Conall reigned but a short time, being ousted by Constantine, who became king of the Picts. Conall fled to the Dalriad Scots, where Constantine's son was in command, and Conall's death in Cantyre is recorded under the year 807, while Constantine continued to rule over the Picts till his death in 820. He was followed by his brother Angus, who died in 834, when Drest, son of Constantine, is mentioned as king, but this was contrary to the rule of the Pictish succession; so one reads of another king besides Drest, namely Talorgan son of Wthoil, who was acknowledged probably by the northern Picts. This was an opportunity for another attempt on the part of the Scottic dynasty to urge their claim by force of arms, which was in fact done by one bearing the name of Alpin, king of Scots. In the war which ensued, Alpin was at first successful, but a second battle in the same year was disastrous to him. Dr. Skene finds that tradition points to the Carse of Gowrie as the scene of this Alpin's attempt, and mentions Pitalpin, now Pitelpie, near Dundee, as the locality where he was defeated, and he calls attention to a Rathalpin or Alpin's Fort, now Rathelpie, near St. Andrews, as a possible indication that Fife was the province in which he established himself after his success at the beginning of the contest. If that be so, it seems to shew that the interests of the Scottic dynasty had been making progress there since the time when Angus had thought it expedient to establish the bishopric of St. Andrews. It probably means also that the language of the Scots, namely Goidelic, had been gaining ground. It had doubtless been rapidly becoming dominant in Gowrie and Athole, and its spread in Fife may have been helped by settlements of Goidels there; for the time from which the Clann Conaill Cirr dated in Fife is not known, so that we may provisionally reckon them, for instance, among the factors in the propagation of Goidelic speech beyond the Forth. The reign of Drest and Talorgan brings the story down to the year 836; then follows Uven, that is doubtless *Owein*, son of the Ungust or Angus who had died king of the Picts in 834; and, as Owein's accession was not according to the rule of the Pictish succession, the northern Picts had probably another king. Years before Owein became king of the Picts, he was ruler of Dalriada; it was there also he seems to have died, namely, in an attempt to repel the Danes. The latter were followed—more correctly speaking, perhaps, assisted—by Kenneth, son of that Alpin the Scot who was defeated and slain in 834. Kenneth accordingly got possession first of Dalriada and a few years afterwards of the kingdom of Alban: the year of his triumph is regarded as 844.

From the advent to power of Kenneth mac Alpin and a Goidelic dynasty, the spread of their language must have proceeded at a rapid rate during their two centuries of more or less continuous rule; and what traces there may be discovered in Scotch place-names of the supercession of Brythonic and Pictish speech by the Gaelic of Kenneth's adherents, is a question deserving of the attention of the philologists and antiquaries of Scotland. I will, however, not dwell on it here, as it is enough for my purpose that in most of the country from the southernmost point of Galloway to the Tay, and a certain distance beyond that river's main stream, the Anglian speech, which you call Broad Scotch, superseded a Goidelic language, not a Brythonic one, at any rate to any considerable extent. So far, then, as this is concerned, one expects a certain amount of uniformity in the Scotch dialects, and one actually finds it, until one proceeds to leave the watershed of the Tay on the way towards Aberdeenshire, where the difference of dialect can escape nobody. This, I take it, represents an ancient state of things: here the language superseded by English among the mass of the people was not Gaelic, but the Pictish of the descendants of the ancient Tæxali; or, at any rate, Pictish had been prevalent there much more recently, and left far fresher features of its habits of pronunciation surviving than in the other districts where English made conquests. The corner of the country represented by the earldoms of Buchan and Mar figure comparatively little in the early history of Alban. So Aberdeenshire may well have been one of the last districts in which the Pictish language survived, and next to it the country this side of the Mounth adjoining Aberdeenshire, and reaching south as far perhaps as Dundee and the Firth of Tay. Let us, then, consider the Aberdeenshire dialect for a moment: can anything Pictish be fixed upon in that dialect? I am inclined to think there can; and I would begin with a question which passed my understanding when I first heard an Aberdeenshire farmer hailing a neighbour with the words: *Foo's a' wi' ye?* This, as I afterwards learned, would be in English, How is all with you? And owing to forgetting that *far* is 'where' in Aberdeenshire, I completely missed the point of a pithy after dinner speech in which the speaker triumphantly said, *Tak awa' Aberdeen an' twal' mile roon' an' far are ye?* But my purpose of comparison would be still better answered by instancing the stock question, *Fa fuppit the fite fulpie?* in which we have *f* no less than four times for the *wh* of the equivalent English, 'Who whipped the white whelpie?' But why, it may be asked, do I fix on that *f* as Pictish? In the first place it is known from other sources that the non-Aryan aborigines of these islands treated the nearly related consonants *w* and *v* differently from the Celts, when they made Dovinia into Duibhni, and Ever into Ebher in the south-west of Ireland, and the Δηούανα of Ptolemy into a form yielding the name *Daven* in *Loch Daven*. I am here tempted also to introduce a Galloway name, though there are several reasons for laying no stress on it: when English finally conquered that district, the language which it superseded was not Pictish but Goidelic; but if you will recall the earlier history of the Picts of Galloway, you will remember that they were for a long time subject to the rule of the Angles of Northumbria, who not only formed the secular rulers there, but also had a succession of bishops at Whithorn, the old Church of St. Ninian, better known to ecclesiastical historians as Candida Casa. There, then, the English of the ruling Angles came probably into direct contact with the Pictish of the subject race, and what was the linguistic result? I cannot answer that question in full, but only just enough for my present purpose; to wit, the English name Whithorn became Futern, as the name figures in Irish literature. That form may possibly be regarded not so much as the result of a Goidelic modification as of a Pictish habit of pronunciation which made English *wh* into *f*, whether Pictish happened to be the vernacular on the Solway or near the Mounth. The same dialect is even more sharply distinguished by its thin vowels,[*] as

---

[*] For calling my attention to this I have to thank Dr. Murray, and on turning to his book on 'the Dialect of the Southern Counties of Scotland' (London, 1873), I find that his conclusions and mine as to the dialect beyond the Tay, supplement one another in a striking manner; his map would serve the purposes of my theory, while the latter finds in Pictish the defining cause, which Dr. Murray's data did not suggest. Roughly speak-

for instance when in Aberdeenshire *do* and *moon* become *dee* and *min*. This likewise is probably to be ascribed to the influence of the long extinct Pictish: at any rate Goidelic phonology has no explanation to offer of any kind.

Finally, enough and more than enough has been said in this lecture to convince you how difficult it is to trace the early spread of Goidelic speech in the Cisgrampian area of ancient Alban: the kernel of this difficulty may be put into the question, When was the first Goidelic-speaking community settled on the banks of the Tay? I have attempted to answer it, but in a very lame fashion, by referring it vaguely back to the time of Aidan the Dalriad Scot and his Miatic War. Supplement this by the probable fact that the clergy of the Columban Church also formed propagators of the Goidelic speech of the Scots, and under the conditions I have suggested, perhaps I may be admitted to have done the best I could; but it will occur to some that these conditions have never before been laid down, and that the difficulty, therefore, which I have been trying to solve, has never before been discussed. That is true, and one would search in vain for any treatment of it in books on the history of Scotland. This is because their authors assume that the Picts spoke a Celtic language, that they were in fact Aryans. If writers holding that view differ among themselves, it is simply on the question whether the Picts were Goidelic or Brythonic, whether they were more like the Irish or the Welsh. But just as the Basque language is crammed full of words borrowed from the surrounding dialects of Romance, so doubtless Pictish in its last stages was full of Celtic loan-words. Nevertheless it is by means of those loan-words that historians usually try to settle the Pictish question. How futile this must be, can be shown from the case of a language whose vocabulary is homogeneous as compared with Basque: I allude to Welsh, which however contains a comparatively small number of words borrowed from Latin; but when it was tried to

---

ing, the western boundary may be represented thus: from the junction of the counties of Perth and Forfar on the Firth of Tay draw a line to the east of Glamis, to the west of Forfar and on to Clova, whence it should join the Highland Boundary and approximately follow it to the Moray Firth near Nairn.

prove that Welsh was an Aryan language, the first attempt was based, I believe, almost entirely on words which were found, on examination, to have been drawn from Latin. Here the attempted proof was no proof, though the conclusion was true; but in the case of Pictish not only is the attempted proof worthless, but in my opinion the conclusion drawn by means of it is wrong. The Picts, whatever they were, were no Celts, and in the next lecture I hope to return to them as a race, which, however brave and hardy, cannot be called Aryan.

JOHN RHYS.

CERTAIN NATIONAL NAMES OF THE ABORIGINES OF THE BRITISH ISLES.

NOW that we have gone through a certain amount of detail, we are in a position to return to the further consideration of some of the most important national names associated with these islands. You have already heard something of Scots and Picts, of Ivernians and Cruithnians; but there were other names which were once widely spread, and one of them makes its appearance in Ireland, in South Wales, and up here in the neighbourhood of the Forth. In the Welsh Chronicle, known as the Annales Cambriæ, and written in Latin, St. Davids, in the south-west corner of Wales, is called Moni, which is in Welsh Mynyw, made in Irish into *Muine* or *Kill Muine*. The traditional Latin, however, for Mynyw is Menevia, and not Moni, which was clearly a form derived from an old Irish source. Further, in the Welsh Chronicle it is not simply called Moni, but Moni Iudeorum, just as if it had been called after a settlement of Jews. That is, however, merely an accident, and I take the name to imply a native form, Iudeu, which appears as the designation, or rather one of the designations, of a people in these islands. A life of St. David describes a contest between him and a certain chieftain near St. Davids, called Boia. He is termed a Pict, and sometimes a Scot; he probably came, or his ancestors before him had come, from the south of Ireland, and he may well be supposed to have been one of the people who gave rise to the designation in the Chronicle for St. Davids, namely, Moni Iudeorum, the authenticity of which is favoured by the fact of its coming from an Irish source, as an Irish writer had less temptation to err, than a Welsh one, in respect of invaders from Ireland. In that island the name figures in literature as *Ith*, genitive *Ithe*, as in *Mag Ithe*, 'the Plain or Field of Ith,' a name applied to several localities in Ireland. They were usually supposed to be so called after a certain ancestor named Ith. Now, as all the peoples of ancient Erinn were commonly regarded as descendants either of Emer or of Erem, there was no room left for him, but he was somewhat inconsistently allowed to remain as an uncle to the twin ancestors; several Ithian tribes figure in Irish history, and to them belonged the O'Driscols, whose territory consisted of the south-west of what is now the county of Cork. In Scotland we have the name of *Ith*, possibly in that of the Island of Tiree, which Adamnan calls *Terra Heth*, of which allied forms occur drawn from other sources. The name Mag Ithe enters into Irish mythography pretty largely: thus the first battle fought in Ireland, namely, between Partholon and his foes, took place on a Mag Ithe, and the contest between the powers of light and the demons of the cold and the damp that blight the cornfield is also fought out on a Mag Ithe. So well known, indeed, seems to have been this name that it found its way into the literature of the ancient Norsemen, who plundered these islands in the eighth, the ninth, and the tenth centuries, for when the Eddic poem of the Volospá makes the Anses, after their grand disaster, reappear in a new order of things, the scene of their meeting is a place called the Field of Ith:—

'I behold Earth rise again with its evergreen forests out of the deep; the waters fall in rapids; above hovers the eagle, that fisher of the falls. The Anses meet on Itha-plain, they talk of the mighty Earth-serpent, and remember the great decrees, and the ancient mysteries of Fimbul-ty.'

The form implied in the Welsh Chronicle was Iudeu, and I mentioned that this name is also found associated with this part of the island, so a few words must now be devoted to it. It is right first to state, however, that it occurs in a Welsh poem called the Gododin, which is one of the most obscure compositions within the range of Welsh literature, so that nobody must be surprised at a very considerable difference of opinion as to the meaning of the passage in which the name occurs. The lines run as follows:—

> ' Tra merin iodeo trileo
> Yg caat tri guaid fraidus leo
> Bribon a guoreu bar deo.'

This has been rendered by Mr. Thomas Stephens, in his posthumous *Gododin*, thus:—

> ' While there was a drop they were like three lions in purpose;
> In the battle, three brave, prompt, active lions.
> Bribon, who wielded the thick lance,' etc., etc.

All that can be said in favour of this translation is that most of us have probably known lions of the kind described by Mr. Stephens; but the fact that in order to render three lines of seven syllables each he gives us English ones respectively of 14, 10, and 8, is sufficient to raise a strong suspicion that the translator was hopelessly guessing the sense of a passage which he could not render word for word. It would, however, be hardly fair to criticise another without giving one's own guesses: I make the passage to mean something like this:

> ' Over the Firth of Iodeo brave
> In war thrice a raging lion
> Bribon wrought the wrath of God.'

Without going into details, I may say that my rendering, such as it is, is literal, and makes the poet compare his hero to a raging lion, making three death-spreading charges on the ranks of his enemies: this he calls executing 'the wrath of God.' I take *merin* to mean *marina* as a late Latin word for an estuary or stormy frith, and Merin Iodeo would accordingly apply to the Firth of Forth, which is called in an old Irish document, quoted by Reeves in his *Culdees* (p. 124), Muir n-Giudan, the Sea of Giuda or Giude. But the genitive *Giudan* in that form was probably more English than Goidelic, and the whole might have been in the Latin of Bede *Mare Giudi*, for he has an *Urbs Giudi* situated in the Firth of Forth. Bede's *Giudi* is undoubtedly to be identified with Nennius' *Iudeu*, whether or not Bæda's town was the same as that which

Nennius had in view. The latter speaks of it in connection with the war between Penda and Osuiu. The latter is compelled to give up the wealth which he had with him in the town called Iudeu to Penda, who distributed it among his allies, the kings of the Brythons; and this, says the writer, is *Atbret Iudeu.* That term would seem to mean the indemnity of Iudeu, that is to say the indemnity paid by Iúdeu. All this agrees very well with the supposition that *Iudeu* meant some of the Picts; and then when the Brython spoken of by Aneurin, was wreaking 'the wrath of God' on his foes beyond *Merin Iodeo*, it means that he was fighting against the Picts beyond the Forth, and for *Merin Iodeo* we have only to substitute a name of the Firth of Forth well-known to Scotch history, namely, Scottis See and Scottewattre.* In any case Iudeu was a widely spread name, as we have already seen in tracing it from Erinn to Menevia, to Tiree and the neighbourhood of the Forth.

The name Pict has already been unavoidably mentioned more than once in these lectures, but I wish now to devote a few further remarks to this national appellation of an ancient people of Britain. But this, perhaps, may seem to you to beg the question, for the question, or at any rate one of the questions, which the word Pict raises, is this: did any people call themselves Picts, or was it merely a nickname given by the Romans and the Roman provincials to a people whom they wished to indicate as *picti* or painted men? That question then resolves itself to this: is the word Pict the Latin word *pictus* or not? It is worthy of note at the outset that the word, whatever it may have meant, is hardly to be severed from the name of the Pictones of ancient Gaul, who have left their name to Poitou and Poictiers: in fact the Picts appear to have been themselves called Pictones.† But the name Pictones is not Latin, nor can it well be a Celtic formation from the Latin *pictus*, for the Pic-

---

* So in the 'Description of Scotland' (A.D. 1165) printed in Skene's *Chron. of the Picts and Scots*, p. 136: it corresponds to an O. English nominative, Scotta wæter.

† See Windisch's article entitled *Keltische Sprachen* in Ersch & Gruber's Encyclopædia, xxxv. 136, and Müller's *Ptolemy* (Paris, 1883), i. 94.

National Names of the Aborigines of the British Isles. 103

tones of Gaul were outside the Roman province when Julius Cæsar came there; and this was at a time when the Latinization of Celtic names cannot have proceeded beyond the limits of Roman sway. So the name of the Pictones and their city of Pictava were not Latin, and so far there is no reason to suppose that the probably kindred form which the Romans treated as Pictus, plural Picti, was Latin either. The word is familiar here in Scotland in its various forms, one of which I understand to be Pecht, and it is hard to believe that it is merely a term borrowed from Latin literature. We may go further and state that on the historical side, so to say, there is very good evidence that Pecht cannot have been derived from the Romans, and that is, the testimony of Norse literature. When the Norsemen approached the northern shores of Britain, they seem to have called Caithness and Sutherland the land of the Pechts or Petta-land, so that the sea washing its northern shores became to them the Pettalands fiorth, or the Firth of the Land of the Pechts; but when they proceeded towards the south, that is to the Hebrides, they came to what they called Scottaland's fiorth, or the Firth of the land of the Scots, the land, that is to say, of the Dalriad Scots, who had extended themselves far north of Argyle by that time. Similarly, when on the east side, the Norsemen reached the Dornoch Firth, they may have come across Picts who had linguistically become Goidels, that is, in other words, ceased to count for them as Picts at all. Now, is it likely that the Norse pirates, approaching the extreme north of this island, came there knowing that the Romans had, in their own tongue, nicknamed the inhabitants of that portion of it *Picts* or painted men? It is far more probable that they learned the name of the Pechts from the islanders of the Faroes, the Shetlands, or the Orkneys, or else from the inhabitants of the mainland themselves.

The Pechtland, which the Norsemen made into Pettaland, is the name which has yielded the modern form Pentland, as applied to the sea on the coast of Caithness, and this must recall to you the name of the Pentland Hills; but the identity of form is a mere coincidence. At any rate, it is hard to believe it to be anything more; for it is very irregular to make Petta-land into Pentland, with an inexplicable *n* in the first element of the compound, so that it would be too much to ask one to believe this irregularity to have exactly reproduced itself at the two extremes of the northern kingdom. As to the name of the Pentland Hills, it occurs sometimes without the *t*,* and this probably brings us nearer to the original, which was possibly a Brythonic compound beginning with the word *pen*, 'a head, end, or top.' In that case the *n* belonged originally to the name of the Hills; and whether sailors from the south of Scotland may not have made some such a form as Pettland into Pentland, thinking they had come across a name already familiar to them, I cannot say, as I am ignorant with regard to the later history of the name of the Firth. But we have here two fixed points, the Norse Pettaland and the modern Pentland, the former of which, involving Pecht, 'Pict,' reduced to *Pett-* by the usual Norse process of assimilating the consonants, proves that the Norsemen found the people of the northern extremity of the island called Pechts. The name applied, doubtless, in this instance, to the representatives of Ptolemy's small tribes of the Lugi, Smertae, Decantae, Cornavii, Carnonacæ, and possibly others; not that there is any reason to suppose that it was by any means confined to them. Moreover, the Norse use of the word serves to bring out clearly a distinction between the Pechts, who probably still spoke their own native tongue, and the Goidelicizing Scots, who had extensively spread their language along the western coast, and possibly across country to Inverness.

So much as to the historical impossibility of identifying the word Pict or Pecht with the Latin *pictus*: there is also a phonetic difficulty, which is still more decisive. Not only was the

---

* For instance, in Fordun's *Chronica Gentis Scotorum*, as edited by Dr. Skene (Edinburgh, 1871), vol. i., p. 284; and at p. 292 he gives the spelling *Pentheland*. The *tl* of the present spelling probably got a footing in the name as a sort of representation of the sound written *ll* in Welsh, which Englishmen frequently imagine to be *thl*. The like is probably the history also of the *tl* in another name in these parts, that, to wit, of *Pencaitland*.

Norse word Pett, and the Early English Pect, but the Welsh was Peithwyr (in the plural), which occurs in the Book of Taliessin. This Peith-wyr is a compound, meaning literally Pict-men, and the syllable *peith*, which represents Pict, is to be found also in the Gododin, where allusion is made to *Wid*, son of *Peithan*. Now, Wid is a well-known Pictish name, and Peithan seems to be a derivative from the word for Pict. The name Peithan also occurs in *Inis Peithan*, 'Peithan's Isle,' a name given in the twelfth century manuscript of the *Liber Landavensis*, to a place in the diocese of Llandaff; and there we are probably to trace it to the conquest of the coasts of the Severn Sea by men from the south of Ireland. With this appearance of *Peith* in a man's name may be compared compounds such as Pect-helm, in which the Angles ruling over the Galloway Picts sometimes indulged. Lastly, some of the translations of Geoffrey of Monmouth into Welsh seem to prove that *Pictavia*, meaning the country of the Picts, had a Welsh form *Peitheu*, or *Peithyw*, or *Peithaw*, which they confounded, under the form *Peitaw*, with the Continental Poitou: the former, according to Geoffrey, was the realm of Melwas, whose subjects, if we follow his story, were the Picts of the North, though, in point of fact, the country whence they came must have been the South of Ireland, that is, supposing the Melwas story to involve a historical element. Now, the Welsh forms with *peith* cannot be derived from a form Pict: it must be Pect-, which is favoured by the Scotch Pecht, the Anglo-Saxon Peohtas, and the Norse Petta-. Though the Welsh form is utterly at variance with the Latin one *Pictus*, there is, as will be seen later, evidence of an Irish form with *i*; but whether you suppose the first syllable as heard by the Romans to have been Pict (Picht) or Pect (Pecht), the difference was scarcely so great as to have prevented them from identifying the word with the Latin participle *pictus*. Whether the same influence of a mistaken etymology is to be detected in the spelling of the name of the Pictones of the Continent is not clear; but the better spelling of that name is vindicated by the *oi* of the French Poictiers and Poitou; for this diphthong comes from an *ē* which is actually found in Ptolemy's

Πηκτόνιον Ἄκρον, a promontory somewhere on the coast of Poitou. On the Continent, then, the vowel proves to have been not an *i* but an *e*, which the Romans, following Latin analogy, would be led to lengthen before the consonantal combination *ct*. In the Brythonic dialects it remained short, so that here we set out from *Pect*.

The name was, as already surmised, owned by the aborigines of North Britain; but I fancy that I detect traces of it also in Ireland, namely, in the form Cecht with its *p* changed into *c*, which is known to have been done in a small number of borrowed words like *caisg* for *pascha*, 'passover or Easter,' and the like. Cecht, however, only occurs as part of the proper names Dian Cecht and Mac Cecht. The former, Dian Cecht, literally means the Swift one of Cecht, and it was borne by a remarkable character in Irish legend, which makes him the great physician of the Tuatha Dé Danann. The other, namely, Mac Cecht, whose designation means Son of Cecht, was the name of one of the three kings ruling over Eriun when the Milesians came and conquered them; and it was Mac Cecht who had to wife the Queen whose name Fodla was mentioned in a previous lecture as a name forming part of that of Athole, in its older form of Ath-Fodla. Another Mac Cecht figures very prominently in the tragic story of the death of Conaire Mór, where he acts as his king's swift servant in all kinds of emergencies. The two Mac Cechts are not identified in any way in Irish literature, though it may be that at bottom the two stories are versions of one and the same event, whether of history or myth.

Unless I am mistaken, this vocable occurs in place-names in Scotland, namely, in the form of Keith (written also Keth, to wit, by Fordun), as in Dalkeith and Keith Humbie, on this side of the Firth of Forth, Inverkeithing (written *Inverkeithin* by Fordun) on the other side of it, and Inch Keith in the middle of it, also Keith Inch at Peterhead, Keith Hall at Inverurie, and the town of Keith in the county of Banff. The phonetic treatment of *ch* in these instances would be much the same as in *Alyth*, for the older form *Aleecht*, occurring in the Life of St. Modwenna. The Welsh form directly corresponding to Cecht is, as already suggested, Peith, liable to be made into Paith in Modern Welsh: two instances of it are known to me in Cardiganshire, one in Dyffryn Paith, 'the Vale of Paith,' and the other in Peithnant, 'Peith Brook,' one of the tributaries of the Rheidol; and possibly *Peithyll*, near Aberystwyth, may be of the same origin. These names suggest the question, who the Pict was that was here meant: was it the Pre-Celtic native of that district or an invader from the North? Probably neither, but the Pict from the South of Ireland who left his name to the Pict's Isle, called in Irish, *Inis Picht*, now corrupted into Spike Island, in Cork harbour. His was the race represented by Boia at St. Davids, and, on the other side of the Severn Sea, by such enemies of Arthur's as Melwas and his men, so far as they belonged to history. Besides the Cecht to which Keith and Peith seem to point, Irish glossaries give a vocable *cicht*, which they explain to have meant 'a carver or engraver.' This I take to be another attempt to Goidelicize Pict or Picht, and I further gather from it that there was a tradition that Pict meant one who carves or cuts; but in what sense it would be hard to say, though I should suggest it to have been in that of 'a great slaughterer or mighty warrior.'* In any case, the name was doubtless meant by those who bore it, to be complimentary to them. This, though a mere hypothesis, will be found to explain two or three other important names to be discussed as we proceed.

Such are the reasons which compel me to give up the idea of connecting the name of the ancient Picts with the Latin participle, and in one respect I regret having to do so; for if, as you must see, we could accept the Latin etymology, then there would be no difficulty in answering the question what the name meant: it could not have been other than painted or tattooed, and one could at once quote Claudian's vivid description of the Roman legionary scanning the figures punctured

---

* This was perhaps the first meaning, and that of *carver* merely what it took in the hands of a glossary-maker influenced by the belief that the Picts were so called from their tattooing themselves.

with iron on the body of the fallen Pict at his feet: the lines are familiar to all readers of Latin literature :

> 'Venit et extremis legio prætenta Britannis
> Quæ Scotto dat fræna truci, ferroque notatas
> Perlegit exsangues Picto moriente figuras.'

At first sight one might be inclined to suppose that the poet was representing a fact in his allusion to the tattooing, but unfortunately we are not warranted in supposing that he drew his inspiration from any deeper source than the popular etymology of the name Pictus, interpreted as a Latin word. If, then, Claudian's words are to be discarded in this way, what evidence, you may ask, is there left that the Picts habitually discoloured their skins? There is no evidence, so far as I know, that they did so, or did so to a greater extent at any rate than their neighbours, and this last qualification is of importance. For we know from Cæsar's Commentaries that the Brythons of southern Britain painted themselves with woad for battle; and from Pliny that their women painted themselves black as Ethiopians for certain religious ceremonies. Nay, one might add that, as late as the fifth century, there were Saxons who painted themselves blue—at any rate if we may trust Sidonius, bishop of Clermont. In all this there is nothing to surprise us, as there are Saxons even now, and Celts too, for the matter of that, who think it nice to have recourse to painting: our sailors adhere to the old custom of tattooing, while the fair sex show their superior taste in contenting themselves with a less glaring hue fixed less deeply in the skin. But the choice of red, of whatever shade, is not to be supposed modern or even comparatively modern, as the finding of pellets of a certain red pigment in some of the most ancient burial mounds of Britain is supposed to indicate. The friends of the departed dandy took care to provide him wherewithal to make a decent appearance among his peers in the other world, that other world being supposed to be much like the present one: the paint would be required there because, as it is urged, it was required in this.

One might, of course, be told that the Picts tattooed themselves, whereas the ancient Brythons of Cæsar's time only painted themselves for battle or ceremonial functions; or else that the latter having given up wholly the luxury of paint in the course of their imitation of Roman fashions during the Roman occupation, it was retained by the Picts, so that it became one of their conspicuous characteristics. All this would be intelligible, but where are the facts? I cannot think of any except one, and that is one which makes for the contrary view. I allude to the negative testimony of Gildas, who was, as already pointed out, a Brython who hated both Picts and Scots. He speaks of them as 'tetri Scottorum Pictorumque greges, moribus ex parte dissidentes, sed una eademque sanguinis fundendi aviditate concordes, furciferosque magis vultus pilis, quam corporum pudenda, pudendisque proxima, vestibus tegentes.' He remarks, as you will have noticed, on the hairyness of their faces, and he takes care to notice the absence of the breeks, still supposed to characterize Highlanders, but never a word does he say of paint or tattoo, though nothing could have pleased him more than to expatiate on any trait or custom of theirs which would have enabled him to hold them up to ridicule or detestation. To my mind this silence on the part of Gildas, this negative evidence of his, is proof positive that neither Picts nor Scots were in the habit in his time of discolouring their skins to any greater extent than his own people and neighbouring nations.

The word Cruithne, which passes as the Goidelic equivalent of Pict, would seem to be a Celtic word, and a late Irish scribe explains it as identical in its connotation with the name Pict, according to his interpretation of the latter, for he says that the Cruithni were so called from the *crotha*, (plural of *cruth*, 'form') or forms of animals which they had painted on their bodies. This is probably based on the common interpretation of the other word Pict. It does not, however, follow of necessity that two names of one and the same people had one and the same meaning. At first sight Dugald MacFirbis might be thought right in deriving Cruithne from *cruth*, as it goes on all fours with the Welsh equivalent Prydein or Prydyn, meaning Scotland, or rather Pictland, and derived from *pryd*, 'form,' which is the exact etymological equivalent of the Irish *cruth*. But, in the first place, it by no means follows that Cruithne meant a man with the forms of animals delineated on his skin; for it might just as well be supposed, so far as this etymology goes, that it meant, for instance, a man of form, that is, of goodly form: let us say *formosus*. In the next place there is a preliminary objection of a grave nature to this etymology *in toto*, namely, that it accounts for too few of the elements of the word Cruithne, for it is in fact somewhat the same as if you explained the English word *tinder* by referring to the English word *tin*, whilst leaving entirely out of consideration the old verb *tind*, 'to kindle.' What, then, we want is an etymology that will take into account not the *cruith*, but the *cruithn* of the word *Cruithne*, and the corresponding Welsh *Prydein*. Unfortunately there is, so far as I know, only one Celtic word that could be of any help to us, and that is the old Irish word for wheat, namely, *cruithnecht*, now written *cruithneachd*, and *curnaght*, in Highland and Manx Gaelic respectively. It probably means simply 'that which is reaped or cut,' and comes from the same root as Lithuanian kertù, 'I cut.' Old Bulgarian chrŭtati, 'to cut;' Sanskrit kart, 'cut, hew,' kartana, 'the act of cutting,' and kartanī, 'a pair of scissors or shears.' If this, then, be approximately the etymology of the word, and if the term Pict involved a reference to carving or cutting, it is but natural to infer that *Cruithne* only acquired the force of a national name as a rendering into Celtic of the native name Pict. Further, in case the word *Scottus* be of Celtic origin, as I am now disposed to think, it is probably to be regarded as another translation into Celtic of the same Non-Aryan word Pict. It is no objection that both translations would have to be admitted as of very old standing, dating, perhaps, so far back as the time when first a Pict began to learn a Celtic language.

This is especially the case with Cruithne, for not only have we its correct equivalents in the Welsh, Prydein and Prydyn, but a trace of it also on the Continent, to which I must for a moment direct your attention. Now there is an Old High German manuscript containing glosses of the beginning of the ninth century: more exactly, the MS. is taken to date before the year 814. It is to be seen at Munich, and it is known to German scholars as the 'Wessobrunner Codex.' Among other things it contains a list of names of places in Latin with glosses in German, thus: *Hybernia* is explained to be Scottono lant, or the Land of Scots, Domnonia to be Prettono lant, or the Land of Brythons, Italia to be Lancparto lant, or the Land of Lombards, and Germania to be Franchono lant, or the Land of the Franks. But the items of special interest here are the following two: Gallia explained to be *uualho lant*, or the Land of the Welsh, for it was the custom of Germanic nations to apply the term Welsh to countries inhabited by Celts, subject to the rule of Rome, and to some countries where the Celtic element was not very conspicuous; but besides Gallia, we have another name interpreted as *uualho lant*, or the Land of the Welsh, and that is given as *Chortonicum*, whence it appears that Chortonicum was another name for Gallia, or a part of it, in the Latin author which the scribe was reading. The *h* in Chortonicum is to be treated like the *h* in Franchono, as characteristic of the scribe's dialect, and *Chortonicum* meant a Latin Cortonicum, to be compared with *Celticum* as applied to the whole Continental domain of the Celts; but what is one to make of the adjective Cortonic which one extracts thus from the Latin author read by the German gloss-writer? The answer to this question was given years ago by one of Germany's greatest philologists, Pott, who died not long ago, highly respected on account of his marvellous learning: he at once perceived that Cortonic could be nought else than the Goidelic adjective Cruithneach, which one is wont to render 'Pictish,' and I have no doubt that he was right. In the language of the Celts of the Q group, the prototype of this word would be an adjective *Qurutanic-os,-a,-on*, into which some of the Pre-Celtic tribes of Gaul would seem to have translated their own national name of Picts or Pictones. Whether the corresponding name was current in the language of the P Celts of the Continent, we have no data for deciding: all we know is, that it was in the language of those of this country, witness the Welsh word Prydyn for the Pictland of North Britain.

This word affords me the opportunity of trying to place before you some very old facts in a somewhat new light. The word Prydyn has an optional form Prydain, written in Medieval Welsh Prydein, and in Old Welsh Pritein, also Priten. Now Prydein or Prydyn properly means the country of the Picts, and, more vaguely speaking, Alban or Scotland beyond the Forth, but Prydein forms a part also of the term Ynys Prydain, 'the Island of Prydein,' which means the whole of this island of Great Britain. It is curious that when the Welsh bethought them of an eponymous hero, deriving his name from this origin, they called him Prydein son of Aedd the Great, which points distinctly away from Welsh. For the name Aedd is not of Brythonic origin, whereas it was common enough as Aid or Aed among Scots and Picts, and it has yielded the derivative Aidan, so well-known as borne by the most active of the early kings of the Dalriad Scots. It is right to say that the eponymous hero, Prydein son of Aedd Mawr, can, so far as I know, only be traced as far back as the Welsh Triads; but it is remarkable that it should point to a non-Welsh origin corresponding to the eponymous Cruithne or Cruithnechan of the Pictish Chronicle. The latter is given, it is true, a father bearing another name, but there can be no doubt that the Welsh version is derived from a genuine Pictish legend, though it would seem to have been lost. The Welsh Prydyn and Prydein may, one or both, have been plurals, meaning *Cruithni* or Picts; but as I am not aware of any evidence to that effect, I shall provisionally treat *Ynys Prydein* as formally meaning the 'Island of Cruithne' in the singular, as if it referred only to the eponymous Cruithne, the theoretic ancestor of the race.

The variants, Prydyn and Prydein point back to a difference of accentuation in the early Brythonic forms, which must have been adjectives, Prutanios, Prutania, Prutanion. *Prydein* and *Prydyn*, when used alone in Medieval Welsh, almost always mean the Pictland of the North, and one can never feel certain that the whole island is referred to unless the word *Ynys* is prefixed: thus, according to the Welsh translators of Geoffrey of Monmouth, Caithness is in Prydein, the rivers of Prydein flow into Loch Lomond, and the Orkneys become Isles of Prydein. The double application of the word to Pictland and to Britain was doubtless found inconvenient, and a distinction was sometimes attempted by making Prydyn mean 'Alban' and Prydein 'Britain.' The rhymes in old Welsh poetry have accordingly been sometimes tampered with, in order to thrust into the composition of ancient authors, a distinction which they had not expressed. However great the inconvenience arising from the two applications of the word Prydein in the middle ages, the usage results quite naturally from the meaning of the term as argued in this lecture: Prydyn or Prydein in the Middle Ages referred to the North where the Cruithni or Picts were still to be found, whereas the term Ynys Prydein must, so far as it concerns its early history, be referred to a far earlier time for its meaning, to a period when the whole island belonged to the Cruithni. As the Brythons invaded it after the Goidels had taken possession, they must have found the name given to it by the Goidels, whom they followed: in other words, Ynys Prydein is but the rendering into Welsh of some such a Goidelic name as Inis Chruithne, 'Island of the Picts,' though that name is not known to Irish literature. It was discarded probably in favour of Alba, genitive Alban, which is no other than the Goidelic form of the Albio, Albionis of ancient authors. Pliny leads one to understand that Albio was even in his time an old-fashioned name for Britain: the Goidels, however, continued its use for many centuries later, for we find Cormac in the ninth century writing of Glastonbury as being in Alba. In fact, the name has not even yet been quite confined to Scotland proper, as I have learned from Manxmen who live in sight of the headlands of Galloway. Pointing to something like a huge mass of wall on the north-western portion of the horizon, I have often asked them what they called it in Manx, and received as the answer words meaning the Mull of *Alba*. This Alba is not associated by them at all with *Albin* 'Scotland,' and the distinction is probably of old standing, as Galloway cannot be said to form a part of Scotland in the older acceptation of the term. The fortunes of the name Albio or Alba may be said to have moved on much the same lines as that of Prydyn, in that the latter came at length to be associated with the northern portions of the island, and this was helped by the importance of the Brythons in the south. The Brythons are in Irish called Bretain, genitive Bretan, representing the originals of the Latin forms, *Britanni*, genitive *Britannorum*, so that the southern parts of Britain came to be described in Irish by phrases which may be rendered into Latin by *apud Britannos, a Britannis*, and the like, while the whole island is never called after them by any name meaning *Insula Britannorum*. Now, as to the relation of the name Ynys Prydein to the hypothetical Inis Chruithne, it would probably be this: the Goidels at first called this country the Island of the Picts or Cruithne, but when they were invaded by the Brythonic Celts and driven to amalgamate more with the ancient inhabitants, they learned to call it Alba; and this would mean that the latter name was that which the ancient inhabitants had been in the habit of giving it. It is needless, accordingly, to say that I make no attempt to guess the meaning of the word Albio or Alba, feeling, as I do, quite satisfied for the present, if the hypothesis here suggested should prove to give a natural and unstrained account of the facts of the case.

The name Ynys Prydein has sometimes been explained as if the second word were identical with the word Britannia, which was in all probability a name made by the Romans from that of the people whom they called *Britanni*. The provincials of this country, however, might be supposed to have borrowed the name from the vocabulary of the ruling Roman; but that supposition can, on phonetic grounds, be shown to be inadmissible, for *ynys* 'island,' Irish *inis*, is a feminine, so that the word following it must soften its initial consonant, which would yield not Ynys Brydain, but Ynys Frydain (*f* is pronounced *v* in Welsh), which is not the case in good medieval Welsh. Similarly, Ynys before Prydain must become Ynys Brydain, though there is a tendency in modern Welsh to restore the radical initial, and so to make it again into Ynys Prydain. Thus, whether you write Ynys Brydain or Ynys Prydain, it is not the Isle of *Britain* literally, but of *Prydein*, a name which has already been shown to relate to the Picts as

Cruithni, so that Ynys Prydein means the Island of Cruithne, or the Pictish race.

We are now in a position to examine to some extent the Latin and Greek ways of designating this country. Since the time of Cicero and Cæsar, Romans who did not wish to follow the Greek habit, gave it the name Britannia, which was a purely Latin formation from the name of the people of the Britanni, whereas authors who wrote in Greek sparingly used Βρεττανία, a form suggested probably by the Latin *Britannia* and the Greek form of the name of the people of the Βρεττανοί. Take, for example, Ptolemy's geography: he speaks of London as a town of Britain, τῆς Βρεττανίας, by which he seems to have only meant the south of the island, as he prefers calling the island as a whole Ἀλουίων, or Alvion. Nevertheless, the ordinary editor makes him speak of the entire group of islands of which Britain was the largest, as αἱ Βρεττανικαὶ Νῆσοι. Are we, then, to infer that he extended the sway of the Βρεττανοί to Ireland? That seems highly improbable, and the explanation is to be sought in another direction; for it is the later scribes and the more sterile editors that put the word Βρεττανικαί in the geographer's mouth. We have, in fact, to go back to our books and learn our lessons better: we have to spell them out carefully, beginning with the best manuscripts of Diodore, Strabo, and Ptolemy. What do we then find? Why, that the manuscripts do not agree among themselves in reading Βρεττανικαί: the word, whatever it was, is found to begin with π, not β, far too often, as pointed out by Prof. Windisch, for that variant to be regarded as a mere accident. Thus Carl Müller, the most recent editor of Ptolemy, has been convinced that he must admit Πρεττανικαί into his text as the best reading, which he finds established by the quotations made by the later geographer, Marcian, and the Byzantine writer Stephanus. Müller considers the case to be much the same with regard to Strabo and Diodore; for he finds the form with π in the best manuscripts of both authors, and, as regards modern editors, he is able to quote on his side the great name of Dindorf. Now Ptolemy, speaking of the whole island, called it Ἀλουίων, at the same time that he spoke of the whole group of islands as αἱ Πρεττανικαὶ Νῆσοι, while Strabo had a habit of calling Britain ἡ Πρετταντκή, and Marcian alludes to Britain and Ireland as the Two Prettanic Islands. This adjective had absolutely nothing to do, in point of etymology, with the name Βρεττανοί 'Brythons,' and Βρετταυία as the name of their portion of the island, in Latin respectively *Britanni* and *Britannia*.

Nothing, however, could be more natural than for the adjective mentioned as Prettanic to come under the influence of those names and to be inextricably confounded with them by the scribes, who found the means of giving their error expression in the spelling by substituting β for π in Πρετταντκή and Πρεττανικαί: in other words the substitution of β for π in these names was entirely due to the other names, Βρεττανοί and its congeners. But is that likely to have been the entire extent of the error? This raises another question, namely, that of the origin of the word Prettanic, as to which, however, there can I think be no serious doubt that it is derived from the same source as the Welsh word Prydein, Old Welsh Pritein and Priten, and the Goidelic *Cruithne*: in fact, Prettanic is approximately the Gallo-Brythonic equivalent of the Goidelic adjective Cruithnech, later Cruithneach, 'Pictish, a Pictish man or Pict.' If that be so, one can have no difficulty in showing that even *Prettanic* cannot have been the genuine form, but Prŭtanic. At present, however, I am not aware of that form being attested exactly by any manuscript; the nearest approach known to me occurs in a verse of the Sibyline Oracles, composed, as it is supposed, in the time of the Emperor Hadrian. It reads thus (Book v. 200, Friedlieb's edition):—

Ἔσσεται ἐν Βρύττεσσι καὶ ἐν Γάλλοις πολυχρύσοις.
'Among the Britons and the Gauls rich in gold will be,' etc.

Here the people of this country, or of the British Isles collectively, are referred to in a dative plural which seems to imply a stem *Brutten*, that is to say, subject to the correction of its consonants, a stem Pruten, corresponding not to the adjective, but to the noun *Priten* in Welsh, and *Cruithen*-tuath, 'Pict-land,' in Goidelic. To put it briefly, there is documentary evidence to force the best editors to correct the Βρεττανικαί of the ordinary editions of Ptolemy into Πρεττανικαί, and there is philological evidence that Πρεττανικαί should be further corrected into Πρυτενικαί, or some form of that kind. Subject to this explanation, the Welsh name Prydein of this island, and the cognate Greek names for it and its group, become facts of comprehensive import for the student of ethnology; for they teach him that the people represented by the names, Cruithne, Prydein, and Pict, were once considered by the Celts to have been the inhabitants *par excellence* of these Islands.

It may be worth the while mentioning that Welsh literature preserves two archaic designations of these islands. For not only is the largest of them called to this day *Ynys Prydein*, 'the Island of Cruithne,' but the story of Kulhwch and Olwen in the Red Book, a manuscript of the fourteenth century, speaks of the whole group as 'the Three Islands of Prydein and the three outlying Islands.' These last were, according to Nennius, those of Orkney, Man, and Wight, while the principal Islands, referred to as being also three, were probably Ireland, southern Britain or Britannia in Ptolemy's sense, and Scotland (north of the Forth and Clyde), reckoned as a separate island. These islands of Prydein or Cruithne are virtually the Πρυτανικαὶ Νῆσοι of the Greek writers of antiquity. This is not all, for the Mabinogion of Branwen and Manawyddan, in the same manuscript, speak of Britain as 'the Island of the Mighty,' a term which has found its way into a version of one of the Grail Romances, and the Kulhwch story once calls the whole group 'the Three Islands of the Mighty and the Three outlying Islands,' with the same denotation doubtless as when Prydein was used in the other formula quoted from the Kulhwch. One thing is fairly certain, namely, that the archaic appellation of the Three Islands of the Mighty must be a translation of an older one, a fact which raises the question, what that was. Our Welsh data suggest no other than that of *Teir Ynys Prydein* 'the Three Islands of Cruithne'; and, in case I am approximately right in regarding Cruithne and Prydein as Celtic translations of the word Pict or Pecht in the sense of a cutter, hewer, or a mighty warrior, this appellation of the Islands of the Mighty must be admitted to be fairly suitable.

Here and there in the British Isles the old designation of the Picts may, in some form or other, be expected to have survived down to a comparatively late date. I have already spoken of it in connection with the Pentland Firth, and it has also been instanced from the other extreme, namely, from *Inis Picht* or Spike Island, in the South of Ireland. I may add a conjecture which I have made with regard to another island, namely, Man. A saint mentioned in the Martyrology of Donegal is called Ruisen of *Inis Picht*, and naturally he has been regarded as connected with the Pictish Isle in Cork Harbour. I am, however, as yet unable to find any further information to that effect; but I detect the name Ruisen, well represented in the Isle of Man. It is written in Manx *Rushen*, and it occurs in the following place-names :— 1. The southernmost political division of the island is the Sheading of Rushen, and it contains the Parish of Rushen, which is called in Manx Gaelic 'Christ's Parish of Rushen,' there being another 'Christ's Parish' in the Island. 2. The Castle, from which Castleton takes its name, is called Castle Rushen or Rushen's Castle. 3. Another place in that part of the Island is called Abbey Rushen or Rushen's Abbey. 4. Even if the two last mentioned names could be traced to that of the Sheading or the Parish, which does not appear probable, there remains another, which cannot well have been derived from either, namely, Glen Rushen or Rushen's Glen, a retired valley drained by a river which flows to the sea on the west, some miles to the south of the town of Peel. Here we have indubitable traces of a Ruisen and, among them, of a religious house: may we not suppose, then, that he was the Ruisen of Inis Picht? Should this conjecture prove well founded, we should have an instance of Man being termed in Irish the Isle of the Picts, which would indicate a time after that name had ceased to be applied by the Irish to any of the larger islands of our archipelago.

Precedence having here been given to the name Pict over that of Cruithne and of Scot, the question may be raised what would happen to it in the language of Celts of the Continent supposing them to have become familiar with it at a time anterior to their dropping the consonant *p*. There can be no doubt as to the result eventually. *Pict* must become *Ict*, and as nothing is known about the phonological phenomenon in question, except that it took place some time or other before Celtic names began to reach the authors of antiquity, there is no difficulty of date in the way of our supposing that the Celts did reduce Pict to Ict. In fact, there is reason to think that they did; witness the name of the Island of Ictis located by Diodore on the south coast of Britain, and to the Irish name of the English Channel, which was the Sea of Icht. This last enables one to make an emendation also in the name of Cæsar's port of embarkation for Britain; for the best reading of it (in the accusative) is *Portum Itium*, which I regard as representing an original *Ictium*. Thus *Portus Ictius* was simply the Ictian Harbour from which one was wont to sail across the Ictian Sea to Britain; but this extemporised and somewhat inexact name was, it would seem, destined to be forgotten by the Romans as soon as they became more familiar with the northern coast of Gaul. Be that as it may, it appears, according to the conjecture suggested, that the earliest name known to the Celts for the Channel meant the Pictish Sea, or sea of the Picts, and that is by no means surprising when we bear in mind that the islands severed by it from the Continent were known to them by names which ascribed them likewise to the Picts as the race of inhabitants in possession.

After having made so much of certain names, I may perhaps be asked what is in a name. My reply is that there may be a good deal of history in a name, and that as the geologist can extract the story of the material globe from a study of the layers composing its crust, so can the student of language occasionally extract somewhat of the history of man from the names he has been pleased to give to himself and his surroundings. Here it will suffice to say that the fact of the ancient Greeks having heard these Islands spoken of in terms signifying the Cruithnian or Pictish Islands, and of the Welsh still calling Great Britain by a kindred name, leaves us in no manner of doubt, who, according to ancient Celtic belief, handed down probably from the days of the first Celtic invader's acquaintance with our shores, were the aborigines of Albion and Erinn. It is true the testimony is not the testimony of the rocks: it is the testimony of facts of another order, and according to that testimony the aborigines must have been the eponymous descendants of Cruithne or Prydein, in other words, the Picts. Before the first intruder of Aryan stock had shewn his fair face and blue eyes in the west, the soil of these Islands had belonged for ages untold to the ancestors of the O'Driscols and O'Duibnes, of the Macbeths and MacNaughtons; and if I seem to have paid too much attention in this lecture to the non-Aryan element, it is because the Celt of Aryan origin is supposed to be better known. The Aryan, being now all the fashion, is always with us, and sometimes even a little more than enough.

As these remarks have of necessity been rather desultory and promiscuous, I may perhaps be allowed here to state briefly the purport of some of them, and one or two of the conclusions to which they point.

The non-Aryan names of Britain and Ireland respectively were probably Albion and Iverion: the latter has been retained in *Erinn*, and the former in *Alban*, which has, however, retreated from the southern portion of the Island to the North.

The principal non-Aryan name of the inhabitants of both islands was some prototype of the word Pict, and traces of its use occur not only in Scotland but also in Ireland and Wales.

The national name Pict was early translated into such Celtic names as Cruithne or Prydein, and Scot; also, perhaps, into other tribal names, the connotation of which has been forgotten.

These islands were called the Islands of the Picts, or names to that effect: that was the meaning of the Greek description, Πρυτανικαὶ Νῆσοι, and of Ynys Prydein, as applied in Welsh to Britain, and we seem to have a prehistoric proof of the use of the vocable *Pict* by Continental Celts in the name of the Isle of Ictis and in that of Portus Ictius.

National Names of the Aborigines of the British Isles. 121

Britania is a name which was formed from that of the Britanni, as the Romans at first called the most important people of southern Britain, whom they afterwards learned, from the people themselves, to call Brittones. Britania at first only meant southern Britain, and it has etymologically nothing to do with Prydein and Πρυτανικαὶ Νῆσοι except that its influence caused the latter to be distorted into Βρεττανικαί, so that the correct form disappeared from the manuscripts.

The non-Aryan inhabitants of a part of Gaul, including what is known as Poitou, were known by names closely related to those of Pict and Cruithne: witness Pictones and Chortonicum. So the pre-Aryan occupants of the Gaulish country in question, and those of the British Isles, must have been considered by the early Celtic conquerors to be of one and the same race.

According to the conclusions drawn by the students of ethnology and craniology, the skulls* of some of the descendants of these pre-Aryan aborigines of the British Isles belong to a type found also in the Basque country; and I am inclined to think that in pre-Aryan times a neolithic race, which may be termed Ibero-Pictish, occupied Western Europe from the Straits of Gibraltar to the Pentland Firth and the Danish Islands of the Baltic.

The range of that race might perhaps be more exactly defined by reference to a map† showing the relative positions of the most remarkable megalithic erections of the West, sometimes called druidic. For anything known to the contrary, these structures may be regarded as monuments of the unaccountable energy of the Ibero-Pictish race, whose existence I have ventured to suggest.

JOHN RHYS.

---

* See more especially Huxley's article on 'The Aryan Question and Prehistoric Man' in last year's *Nineteenth Century*, pp. 758-61.

† Such as the map appended by Fergusson to his *Rude Stone Monuments* (London, 1872) and 'designed to illustrate the distribution of Dolmens, and probable lines of the migrations of the Dolmen builders,' or that inserted in Krause's *Tuisko-Land* (Glogau, 1891), and described by him as the 'Verbreitungslinien der megalithischen Denkmale in der alten Welt.'

Also published by Llanerch:

THE BLACK BOOK OF CARMARTHEN
translated by Meirion Pennar

LIVES OF THE SCOTTISH SAINTS
translated by W. Metcalfe

MABINOGION
the Guest translation
with new illustrations
in the Celtic style

ANGLO-SAXON RIDDLES
translated by Louis Rodriguez

SYMBOLISM OF THE CELTIC CROSS
by Derek Bryce,
illustrated by J. Romilly Allen
and others

THORSTEIN OF THE MERE
A SAGA OF THE NORTHMEN IN LAKELAND
by W. G. Collingwood

A HISTORY OF THE KINGS
by Simeon of Durham

From booksellers.
Write for a complete list to:
Llanerch Enterprises,
Felinfach, Lampeter,
Dyfed. SA48 8PJ.